# EVE
## OF
# IDES

*For Gene*

# EVE OF IDES

*A PLAY OF CAESAR AND BRUTUS*

"The Ides of March is come."

*— D. Blixt*

## DAVID BLIXT

Published by
Sordelet Ink

This is a work of fiction. All of the characters, events, and organizations portrayed in this work are either products of the author's imagination or used ficticiously.

## Eve Of Ides

Copyright © 2012 by David Blixt

Cover by David Blixt

All rights reserved. No part of this book may be reproduced in any form by any electronic or mechanical means including photocopying, recording, or information storage and retrieval without permission in writing from the author.

ISBN-13: 978-0615895413
ISBN-10: 0615895417

For information about production rights, visit:
www.davidblixt.com

Published by Sordelet Ink

Inspired by the facts of history,
the plays of Shakespeare,
and the novels of
Colleen McCullough.

For my father

**Al Blixt**

The best man I have ever known

*The first reading of Eve Of Ides was held at the Shakespeare Theatre of New Jersey as part of their 'Lend Us Your Ears' series.*

*It was directed by Rick Sordlet, and produced by Joe Discher, under Artistic Director Bonnie Monte.*

CAESAR – **Edward Gero**
BRUTUS – **Grant Aleksander**
ANTONY – **Michael Rossmey**
VARRO – **Robert Hock**
SERVANT – **Arthur Lazalde**

# FOREWARD

The historian Plutarch writes that, the night before he was assassinated, Caius Julius Caesar attended a dinner party. Also in attendance were his nephew Marcus Antonius (Mark Antony) and the leader of the regicidal assassins, Marcus Junius Brutus.

Eve of Ides explores the relationship betwen Brutus and Caesar, both before and after death. The first act records the events of that fateful dinner the night before the Ides.

The second act is a scene hinted at in Shakespeare's play, but never staged – the second appearance of Caesar's ghost to Brutus.

## DRAMATIS PERSONAE

### IN ORDER OF APPEARANCE

CAESAR – Caius Julius Caesar
SERVANT – an ancient slave in Lepidus' house
BRUTUS – Marcus Junius Brutus
ANTONY – Marcus Antonius
VARRO – Marcus Terentius Varro

# I

MARCH 14, 44 BC

# Act One

### March 14, 44 BC
### Interior Roman House - Evening

*In darkness. Snippets of the Cassius/Brutus dialogue are overcut, creating a cacaphony, with one speech running through clearly.*

CASSIUS *(V.O.)*
Why, man, he doth bestride the narrow world
Like a Colossus, and we petty men
Walk under his huge legs and peep about
To find ourselves dishonorable graves.
Men are some times masters of their fates.
The fault, dear Brutus, is not in our stars,
But in ourselves, that we are underlings.

*The speech then changes to laughter and sounds of a pleasant, slightly rowdy dinner party. It is at a distance, as if in another room.*

*Lights up to discover CAIUS JULIUS CAESAR - 55, aristocratic, tall, fit, balding, smartly dressed - standing at a desk with several papers about him. He reads one while signing another, working furiously. During the whole act,* he is constantly working. The room does not belong to him, so his clutter seems out of place. He takes one sheet over to the window to read by the fading exterior light. Frustrated, he turns up a lamp. He makes several notes, scratches out a line.

CAESAR
(calling) Who's within?

*A SERVANT enters. The sounds from the dining room increase.*

CAESAR
(handing the paper to the SERVANT) Take this to Caius Trebonius at once. Tell him to have it prepared for a vote in tomorrow's meeting.

SERVANT
Yes, Caius Julius. At once.

*Thunder.*

CAESAR
And inform the augers I want sacrifices to keep Jupiter at bay tonight. This storm looks - portentous.

*The SERVANT bows and exits. CAESAR returns to work.*

*BRUTUS enters. He is a man in his middle forties, expensively clothed.*

BRUTUS
A problem, Caesar?

CAESAR
No, merely last minute detritus. Go back, Brutus, enjoy the company.

BRUTUS
I was deputed to find you.

CAESAR
*(snorting)* With all Antony's antics, I'm astonished I was missed.

BRUTUS
The Dictator's absence will always be felt.

CAESAR
And resented. Almost as much as his presence. Go back, Brutus, feast. Lepidus has set a magnificent table.

BRUTUS
For your benefit, Caesar.

CAESAR
*(Writing industriously)* Can't be helped. Directly after tomorrow's Senate meeting, I leave for the kingdom of the Parthians. The ghost of Marcus Crassus will haunt me until I avenge his lost eagles. *(Lays his pen aside and looks at BRUTUS for the first time)* You're sure you won't come? A campaign like this comes along once in a lifetime.

BRUTUS
Not if you are Caesar.

CAESAR
Candidly, even Caesar is excited at the prospect. A truly foreign war, against a rich foe who has bested us once already. Weather, terrain, climate, numbers – all will be against us. The war in Gaul pales in comparison. And then there's the personal stake. I will have the King of the Parthians kneel before dead Crassus' tomb and beg forgiveness.

**BRUTUS**
Terrible. Little though I liked the man… *(shivers)* An airless death frightens me.

**CAESAR**
Then hold your breath until the fear passes.

**BRUTUS**
Face your fear. How very Caesar.

**CAESAR**
We never feel more alive than at the edge of some precipice. *(claps his hands together)* Come, Brutus! Do! Go with me! I would depart all the more willingly with you at my side.

**BRUTUS**
I have duties to perform here. Your own fault, Caesar. You made me Urban Praetor. Under the law, I cannot leave the city.

**CAESAR**
Sulla's law, Brutus, Sulla's law! What one dictator put in place, another can remove. Or simply grant an exemption. Let it be no obstacle.

**BRUTUS**
It wouldn't be a Right Act.

**CAESAR**
*(sighing)* Zeno. When Cato died I hoped never to hear his philosophy again.

**BRUTUS**
Let me rephrase, then. However rigged the elections were, I was voted in by the people in their Centuries. It would be shirking my obligation to Rome to leave the people without their chief judge for the whole term of my year in office. *(CAESAR*

*starts to speak)* No, don't - please, don't make it more difficult. I am not you. I am not martial at heart. As well you know.

CAESAR
Yes. What was it your mother used to tell people when she kept you back from the Campus Martius?

BRUTUS
A weak chest.

CAESAR
But not a weak stomach. Or a weak heart. Your misfortune, Brutus, is that you've never campaigned with me. Cicero is far from being the next Ares, and poor Pompey was past it. Come, see a real campaign.

BRUTUS
I have seen one, Caesar. From the losing side.

CAESAR
Pharsalus was not Pompey's best hour, true. *(grimly)* But neither was it mine. Oh Brutus! Come with me! I'll even bring your brother-in-law, if you like. Little though I love Cassius, he's a brilliant soldier, and his organizational skills almost equal my own. The pair of you can be my senior legates, and we will finally be what we always should have - allies in a great cause.

BRUTUS
*(ruefully amused)* You're not used to 'no', are you?

CAESAR
*(grinning)* Certainly not these days. It's refreshing, in a way. But I would appreciate your company, above all men's. Truly.

**BRUTUS**
I will – think on it, Caesar.

**CAESAR**
You don't have much time.

**BRUTUS**
No. Just tonight. *(beat)* You'll have my answer after the Senate's business tomorrow.

**CAESAR**
Excellent. I'm sure your good sense will rule. You are the most pragmatic of fellows, as well as the gentlest. My darling little Julia always said--

**BRUTUS**
*(interrupting)* Wasn't Antony angling for the senior legate post.

**CAESAR**
What?

**BRUTUS**
I thought Antony was tapped for senior legate.

**CAESAR**
*(grimly)* Antonius is not coming.

**BRUTUS**
You're not taking him?

**CAESAR**
Not if he were Hercules himself. No, I'll leave him with just enough power to satisfy him, with Dolabella and Lepidus to muzzle him.

**BRUTUS**
He was just talking in there just now. He thinks he's going.

CAESAR
He is not. If he doesn't like it, he can jump in the Tiber.

BRUTUS
Caesar, you don't believe the rumors--

CAESAR
It's no rumor.

BRUTUS
Caesar, it's nonsense, just someone's--

CAESAR
It is absolutely true. Antonius leapt the wall to my house in an attempt to murder me.

BRUTUS
No! Surely he just meant to steal a little money. Everyone knows his debts are colossal.

CAESAR
And what better way to pay them than for Antonius to inherit my fortune.

BRUTUS
Better he wasn't your heir, then.

CAESAR
I am of the same mind. But I have no intention of crossing that particular river just yet.

BRUTUS
Crossing rivers has never worried you before. *(beat)* That was unworthy. Forgive me.

*CAESAR looks at BRUTUS with genuine affection.*

CAESAR
Anything, my boy. There is nothing you could ever

do that would disappoint me.

BRUTUS
(uncomfortable) A shame you do not feel the same about Antony.

CAESAR
I wouldn't walk the length of my shadow for Antony. But for you, Brutus, I would walk the Nile and back.

*BRUTUS pours himself some wine, mixing it with water. Suddenly his head comes up.*

BRUTUS
That business in the street today, the soothsayer--

CAESAR
Ha! Yes, old Spurinna puts on quite a show, doesn't he? 'Beware the Ides of March' indeed!

BRUTUS
You think he was paid by Antony.

CAESAR
It does seem likely, doesn't it? Antonius is behind nine-tenths of this 'King of Rome' nonsense. You saw him offer me that idiot crown? Not once, but three times.

BRUTUS
I heard about it. But why would he--?

CAESAR
Perhaps he means to make my death more palatable by turning the public against me.

BRUTUS
Or the nobility. There are rumors - whispers of... men who mean you harm.

CAESAR
*(wryly)* I'm sure.

BRUTUS
The Ides are tomorrow.

CAESAR
*(signing another order)* I know it too well. I'll be up at dawn to officiate the sacrifices to Mars. It's his month.

BRUTUS
You shouldn't have dismissed your lictors. It gives men ideas.

CAESAR
Bodyguards are an admission that there is danger. Caesar will not live in fear. Nor will he be seen to do so.

BRUTUS
Even if it tempts men's lesser natures.

CAESAR
The gods do not test men past their abilities.

BRUTUS
Nor elevate them past their desserts.

CAESAR
Just so. *(pause)* There is something on your mind, Brutus.

BRUTUS
I'm struggling with something, Caesar.

CAESAR
Then please allow me to help. I will happily be the whetstone to your sword.

**BRUTUS**
I've been thinking... it sounds ridiculous to say out loud.

**CAESAR**
So be ridiculous. You may trust me not to laugh.

**BRUTUS**
I've been thinking of the Republic. Of Roma herself.

**CAESAR**
That is far from ridiculous, Brutus. I spend nearly every waking hour in the same contemplation. And I am hardly ridiculous.

**BRUTUS**
No. Wine?

**CAESAR**
Never.

**BRUTUS**
I've never known a man so abstemious. Or is it the taste?

**CAESAR**
I like the taste fine. I do not like how it dulls my mind. Homer had it right. 'Wine can of their wits the wise beguile, make the sage frolic, and the serious smile.' If a man is the sum of his actions, actions require thought. I do not want history judging me based on some alchohol-riddled misstep.

**BRUTUS**
*'In vino veritas.'* They say wine reveals our true natures.

## CAESAR
*(laughing)* Perhaps that's why I am afraid! But drink up, Brutus - you've nothing locked deep in your soul that needs hiding, I'm sure.

*BRUTUS stares at his cup, then sets it aside.*

## BRUTUS
What's that you're signing?

## CAESAR
*(holds up one piece of paper)* This? An order to restore the property to Curio's family - past time. *(holds up another)* This is an execution order for one of Pompey's freedmen who tried to inform on his family. Can't have that. *(holds up a third)* This is a pardon for Africanus' men who came over to us before the battle in Spain.

## BRUTUS
Life and death, with the stroke a pen.

## CAESAR
Mightier than the sword. So tell me, Marcus Junius Brutus - what have you been thinking about Roma and the poor old Republic?

## BRUTUS
I've been wondering when we lost our way. When we stopped being the people we say we are. I've been wondering how the gods will restore the Republic.

## CAESAR
Is she lost? Forgive me, that was facetious. Believe it or not, Brutus, the gods work through me. I am their instrument.

## BRUTUS
Caesar - the Republic cannot be restored by a dictator.

His very existence refutes the notion. Democracy cannot be imposed.

**CAESAR**
You *have* been thinking.

**BRUTUS**
Yes. And I think you're setting a dangerous precedent.

**CAESAR**
Of?

**BRUTUS**
Of - there's not other word for it. Kingship. Of absolute rule. The office of Dictator was created for a time of crisis, a strong leader to run Rome for six months at most, then *step down*. You've turned it into a lifetime appointment.

**CAESAR**
Did I? I thought it was voted by the people.

**BRUTUS**
You are one more step down the path that Sulla pioneered.

**CAESAR**
*(coldly)* I am no Sulla.

**BRUTUS**
No. You are fair where he was foul, in every way.

**CAESAR**
I'm glad you see that. So many of the First Class do not. Despite the fact that Sulla would have had their heads.

**BRUTUS**
But he laid the trap you've fallen into.

**CAESAR**
Trap?

**BRUTUS**
Would you have marched your army on Rome without his example to guide you?

**CAESAR**
Interesting. You're either questioning my nerve or my ingenuity. To be sure, Sulla was - unnatural. But for all that, he was quite the pragmatist. As am I.

**BRUTUS**
I wish I were.

**CAESAR**
I'm glad you are not. Rome needs dreamers just as much as it needs doers. What is Rome, if not a dream? Brutus' Dream. That would be a fine title for a play.

**BRUTUS**
You should write it.

**CAESAR**
I'm afraid I have a different theatrical endeavor in mind. Did you know the Parthians used poor Crassus' head as a prop for a production of the Bacchae? He was dead Pentheus, molten gold still in his throat.

**BRUTUS**
Horrible.

**CAESAR**
When I've won, I have it in mind to stage the same play, with king Orodes in the role. Like for like.

**BRUTUS**
Horrible. Caesar, vengeance doesn't suit you. Instead of Parthia, you should retire and write poetry. You have the knack.

**CAESAR**
What, sitting around a luscious villa in Tusculum and stringing words together? I'm no Cicero. And there's too much to be done! I can't not be doing. I'd die of boredom.

**BRUTUS**
Then you'd die a hero. The man who walked away from power.

**CAESAR**
Ha! Weren't you just warning me of turning into Sulla? He did just that - walked away from power, retired to that luscious villa for games and theatre and remarkably inventive sex for the rest of his days. Yet he is reviled.

**BRUTUS**
Of course he's reviled! He marched a Roman army on Rome! On a defenseless city!

**CAESAR**
As did I.

*Thunder. The rain starts growing in intensity.*

**BRUTUS**
That was different.

**CAESAR**
How? No, how, exactly? Both of us used the military to make a political point.

**BRUTUS**
You were still the general. Technically his march was mutiny.

**CAESAR**
Technicalities are for lesser lawyers, Brutus.

**BRUTUS**
The law is made up of those technicalities.

**CAESAR**
The law is a breathing thing, Brutus. It cannot be static. When the Senate - a few hundred men of birth and wealth, making laws for people they despise - when they make laws that go against the wishes or interests of the people, they abrogate their authority.

**BRUTUS**
Is that how you see the Senate?

**CAESAR**
*(laughing)* I've been a member too long to see it as anything other than what it is - a collection of privileged fools who do nothing and obstruct everything. They'll fight even the most basic, clear-headed notion because it was suggested by their political enemy. As if we were not all Romans! Picking absurd fights to protect some petty private interests, backing so deep into a political corner that my only viable solution is military. Lawmakers with a profound disdain for the law. *That* is how I see the Senate. Whereas you see it as you wish it to be - a just and wise body of men.

**BRUTUS**
The dreamer.

**CAESAR**
And the pragmatist.

**BRUTUS**
Like Sulla. Who waged war on Roma.

**CAESAR**
Not Roma. Sulla never warred against the people of Rome, only the Senate. And after the war he had himself made dictator to ensure there could never again be such strife.

**BRUTUS**
See how well that went.

**CAESAR**
A hit. Is this what's on your mind? After five years, you choose tonight to speak of the Rubicon?

**BRUTUS**
Perhaps I finally see that a river can't be uncrossed.

*The SERVANT enters.*

**SERVANT**
Forgive me, Caius Julius, Marcus Junius. The rain...

*He gestures to the windows. CAESAR waves a hand, and the SERVANT begins closing the window shutters. The rain is still audible. BRUTUS is silent. CAESAR returns to his pile of papers and picks up a sealed letter.*

**CAESAR**
I have a note here from Pompey's son Sextus. Any interest?

**BRUTUS**
A keen interest. He's due a session in my court.

*CAESAR tosses the letter to BRUTUS, along with a golden letter-opener.*

CAESAR
No need to tell me what it says. He's refusing my offer of a pardon.

BRUTUS
A rare exception. Caesar's clemency is famous. I should know - you pardoned me.

CAESAR
Nothing to pardon.

BRUTUS
*(opening the letter and scanning it)* He uses some very salty language - well, he's a natural sailor - but the gist is you can stick your pardon in, ah, a fundamental orifice.

CAESAR
Quite. His father's son.

SERVANT
Oh, Marcus Junius? Your brother Caius Cassius asked me to give you this note.

*BRUTUS lays down the letter and hastily takes the note, tucking it away.*

BRUTUS
Tell him I know what he wants, and he'll have my answer tonight.

*The SERVANT bows and exits.*

CAESAR
You do well not to talk in front of slaves. Pitchers

have ears. So - the Rubicon. What's set that gnat whirring tonight of all nights?

**BRUTUS**
*(turning the golden letter-opener over in his hands)* It's a gnat that pesters every patriotic man.

**CAESAR**
Painting me as unpatriotic. *(BRUTUS opens his mouth)* No, for Jupiter's sake, don't soften it! I've been called far worse.

**BRUTUS**
It's on my mind because - I've been approached...

**CAESAR**
A petition?

**BRUTUS**
*(seizing on the idea)* Yes. In my court.

**CAESAR**
A good one, I hope. It's been too long since we had a sensational murder trial. Who is the accused?

**BRUTUS**
A group of men, businessmen, but honorable, who've had their company usurped by one of the older shareholders.

**CAESAR**
And doubtless the dead man is the usurper. What business are they in?

**BRUTUS**
Armaments.

**CAESAR**
Hmph. I probably know them. No, no names, please. Don't want to be accused of tampering with the

courts. There are enough complaints against me already. Who brings the suit?

BRUTUS
The company's workers. They were devoted to him.

CAESAR
Do they have standing?

BRUTUS
None better.

CAESAR
I see. Have the accused offered any defense?

BRUTUS
They were trying to save the company from ruin.

CAESAR
By murder? They couldn't vote the man out?

BRUTUS
The workers wouldn't allow it. But the company was failing.

CAESAR
A defense of justification, to cover their own weakness. But the case does raise an interesting question: was the company more important than the man's life?

BRUTUS
And your answer is?

CAESAR
No man is indispensable. On the other hand, murder is still murder.

BRUTUS
If you were hearing the case, what would you do?

CAESAR
Let them off, but make them sell their shares in the company. Even if their cause was just, they can't be allowed to profit from their deed.

BRUTUS
So they were justified?

CAESAR
Did I say that? Still, when the pot is broken, all that's left is picking up the pieces. *(arching an eyebrow)* Do I sense a parallel? A parable, even?

BRUTUS
You wouldn't have them killed?

CAESAR
Executing citizens is un-Roman. Freedmen and slaves, yes, if necessary. But I have never advocated death for anyone. You know that.

BRUTUS
I do. You should add another name. Caius Julius Caesar Clemens. That what makes it all more... The chief defendant is the man's son.

CAESAR
Patricide?

BRUTUS
Adopted son. But still, he loved his father.

CAESAR
Yet, for the good of the whole, he slew him. Admirable.

BRUTUS
Abominable! Mouthing words of love, then raising a hand...

**CAESAR**
Why not? A man may simultaneously love his country and attack it. Case in point - the Rubicon.

**BRUTUS**
What? No, that doesn't answer. Caesar, you can't declare war on your own country and simultaneously cloak yourself in patriotism.

**CAESAR**
*(grinning)* Who says I can't?

**BRUTUS**
Caesar, it is impossible to simultaneously love your country and attack it. It's like those wretched men who beat their wives and claim they do it out of love.

**CAESAR**
Not only unpatriotic, but on the level of a wife-beater. You're sweating, Brutus. Is it too warm?

**BRUTUS**
*(setting aside the letter-opener)* You're telling me it's possible to love a thing and fight against it?

**CAESAR**
Not only is it possible, it's likely. A potent emotion, love - it leads to violent upheavals. But I think you're misstating the situation. Like Sulla, I never declared war against Rome. Only the Senate. The Senate is not Rome.

**BRUTUS**
*Senatus Populesque Romanus.*

**CAESAR**
Yes. The Senate *and People* of Rome. The people greeted me with flowers. *(beat. Then, with mocking*

*formality)* Marcus Junius Brutus, as Urban Praetor I appeal to you--

BRUTUS
Please, don't.

CAESAR
I'm quite serious. You're thinking about petitions. Hear mine, and as Rome's Chief Justice, you can decide - patriot, or villain?

BRUTUS
This is neither the time, nor the place...

CAESAR
I'm the dictator. Humor me.

*With a frown, BRUTUS subsides.*

CAESAR
Learned Urban Praetor, my case is thus: as governor of Italian Gaul, I signed treaties with the German and Gallic tribes across our border, making them Friends and Allies of the Roman people. Perfectly legal and correct. One of these allies was attacked by a neighbor, and I went to mediate their dispute--

BRUTUS
With your army.

CAESAR
With *Rome*'s army. Then, having settled them down, I decided it was high time the Gallic people to the West should have treaties as well. So I crossed the border into Gallia Comata.

BRUTUS
Again, with your army. Only this time without any legal pretext.

**CAESAR**
But a great deal of precedent. Many Roman governors have taken their armies when meeting new people. We were peaceful - paid for everything, shed no blood. How was I to know that the Gauls would rise up? And that, when beaten, they would urge other Gallic nations to unite against Rome?

**BRUTUS**
So a one-year governorship became a ten-year war.

**CAESAR**
Which Caesar won.

**BRUTUS**
Which Rome won.

**CAESAR**
No. Caesar. *(beat)* But when the war was over, was I welcomed by the Senate? Was I allowed to enter the city of my birth and receive the acclaim due me? No. Rather your uncle Cato and his unlikely ally Pompey, along with a handful of petty, backward-looking self-immolating fanatics decided to bring me up on charges - treaty-breaking, launching illegal wars, creating new citizens among the Gauls.

**BRUTUS**
All of which charges you could have answered in court.

**CAESAR**
With juries composed of senators. I stood no chance. What would you have had me do, Urban Praetor? Submit to trumped up charges? Given up my name, my property? Sacrificed that thing I prize above all else?

**BRUTUS**
You could have kept your citizenship.

**CAESAR**
At the price of my dignity.

**BRUTUS**
*That's* where you lose the argument, Caesar. You hold your dignity above the honor of being a Roman.

**CAESAR**
Being a Roman, I hold my dignity at the *exact* level of Rome's. Brutus, I am Rome. You are Rome. Cassius, Antony, Lepidus - they're all Rome. Pompey, Cato, Bibulus - they were Rome. Not just Romans. They were Roma herself. It isn't-- it isn't enough to strive and achieve for personal gain or for family. You must add something to the ever-rising monument to Roma's greatness. If, after conquering all of Gaul, I had allowed myself to be sent into exile, it would not only have diminished me. It would have diminished Rome.

**BRUTUS**
You are a wonderful advocate, Caesar. But there is a flaw in your argument. You pretend an ignorance that's beyond you.

**CAESAR**
I beg your--

**BRUTUS**
'How was I to know the Gauls would rise?' You're the greatest military and political mind in the world. Do you expect anyone to believe you didn't know exactly what you were doing?

CAESAR
You admit I stayed within the law.

BRUTUS
If you admit you knew the consequences of your actions.

CAESAR
*(smiling slightly)* Suspected, perhaps. But, Brutus, I was scrupulously proper, within the letter of the law--

BRUTUS
Pardon me, Caesar--

CAESAR
Anything.

BRUTUS
Legal semantics cannot undo your deeds.

CAESAR
If they could, Brutus, I would surround myself with lawyers. In all my life, I've wanted nothing more than to be legal.

BRUTUS
Perfect, you mean.

CAESAR
I do not regard myself as perfect.

BRUTUS
I didn't say you thought you were perfect. I said you want to be. And you won't tolerate anyone around you to be less than perfect themselves. You'd cast aside your own son, if you had one. *(quickly)* Forgive me, Caesar.

**CAESAR**
Don't shy off! One of the problems with being dictator is that no one speaks his mind. Licker-fish and ass-spongers all. They say only what they think I want to hear. What man wants that?

**BRUTUS**
Now who's dreaming? That's the desire of men throughout history - to be perpetually correct in everything they say and do.

**CAESAR**
Well, I've lost that race, haven't I?

*BRUTUS looks at CAESAR curiously, then crosses to the map.*

**BRUTUS**
Once you've beaten the Parthians, Caesar, will you weep?

**CAESAR**
What?

**BRUTUS**
'When Alexander saw the breadth of his domain he wept, for there were no more worlds to conquer.'

**CAESAR**
There is more in me than the conqueror, Brutus.

**BRUTUS**
Then show it. Step down, and be virtuous.

**CAESAR**
Virtuous?

**BRUTUS**
Virtue alone is sufficient for a happy life. A virtuous man cannot be harmed by poverty, illness, war, or

exile. Endurance is a virtue.

**CAESAR**
But passivity is not. To passively endure things is a woman's lot, not a man's. A man must fight injustice, don't you agree?

**BRUTUS**
But how far must a man go? That's what I'm struggling with. And how to go about it? Is it right to battle injustice with injustice?

**CAESAR**
You have my answer.

**BRUTUS**
Yes. To you, injustice justifies any act. Even treason. Even murder.

**CAESAR**
I regret it, but yes.

**BRUTUS**
You have regrets? I thought you were impervious to them.

**CAESAR**
Hardly. *(beat)* You know, in a way the Rubicon was my greatest defeat. In that moment, I lost something. I felt it go, like a broken thing inside me.

**BRUTUS**
What was it?

**CAESAR**
A dream. My dream. Of being the greatest Roman of all time.

**BRUTUS**
You think you're not?

CAESAR
Not the way I wanted. Until that moment, I had done everything properly. Served in the right number of campaigns, held every office in the proper year. I wanted to be consul a second time, then censor, then become an elder statesman, possibly even Leader of the Senate. 'Primus inter pares.' The first among equals.

BRUTUS
Instead you are a god in Ephasus, a king in Aegypt, and Dictator of Rome. Undisputed ruler of the world. It's not enough?

CAESAR
Far too much... *(shaking off his grim thoughts)*. I should thank Lepidus. This is the best dinner conversation I've had in years.

BRUTUS
Something you said-- It reminds me of the story of Caius Popillius Laenas.

CAESAR
Because he faced down the King of Syria alone, with no more than a stick in the sand? Whereas I brought my army with me.

BRUTUS
I didn't mean it as a slight. I was thinking of what Laenas told the king. *(BRUTUS begins acting out the story, placing CAESAR in the role of the king)* Using a stick, he drew a circle around the king, then said, 'Before you step out of that circle give me a reply to lay before the senate.'

'Where is your army?' demanded the king.

'I don't need an army,' answered Laenas. 'Everything that Rome is, ever has been, and ever will be, is standing before you now. I am Rome's army. I am Rome's might. I am Rome.'

CAESAR
And the king turned around and headed back to Syria. Yes, Brutus, exactly. Laenas had a sense of himself in Rome's pageant. So do I.

BRUTUS
Is that the lesson you take?

CAESAR
What else?

BRUTUS
It astonishes me.

CAESAR
What?

BRUTUS
You act as if you know how history will judge you. But what seems right in the moment often turns out to be wrong. How do you make the irrevocable choice? How – how do you cross that river?

CAESAR
I think of what a true Roman would do. Laenas. The two Scipios, Marius. Yes, even Sulla. What Brutus would do. What Romulus would do. In the case of the Rubicon, the answer was plain. Remus mocked the humble walls Romulus had built, so Romulus slew him. His own brother.

BRUTUS
How does that answer? Remus died for doing precisely what you did – he broke the sacred

boundary of Rome.

CAESAR
No. Remus died for *diminishing* Roma.

BRUTUS
Remus broke Rome's law. So did you. What is Rome without law?

CAESAR
Whose law? I ask you, Brutus, whose law? Under the law, all Roman citizens are equal, from the noblest to the meanest, from Brutus to the poorest of the Head Count. But I was not to be afforded that inalienable right. *Inalienable*, Brutus. What they gave to Pompey, they refused to me. Your uncle Cato and the rest held one set of laws for those in their good graces, and another for the men they disdained. And why did I earn their disdain? What was my real crime? Excellence. Great men are no longer allowed to exist, they must be torn down. In their Rome there is no room for superior men. Mediocrity rules. Anyone who dares show himself brilliant, ambitious, and able is not to be tolerated. If they cannot beat him within the rules, well, it must be time to change the rules! That is injustice, plain and simple.

BRUTUS
What you say is true, and rational – and wrong! You broke the law. Damn the circumstances, you broke the law!

CAESAR
It was already broken by other men.

BRUTUS
'They made me do it?' Another fallacy, Caesar. Two

wrongs do not make a right. Besides, who has ever made you do anything you didn't want to?

CAESAR
Are you saying I wanted to cross the Rubicon?

BRUTUS
I'm saying a man is not defined by his enemies, but by his actions. Caesar is far too much his own man to allow himself to be defined any other way.

CAESAR
I take responsibility for my actions. But I also acknowledge the circumstance. Morality in a vacuum is hollow philosophy.

BRUTUS
Being a dreamer, I have to disagree. Morality is like the law - if it changes in different circumstances, it's not worth having.

CAESAR
My point exactly. If the law-makers break their own laws, what's an honorable citizen to do?

BRUTUS
Wage civil war, obviously.

CAESAR
A very civil civil war. What blood did I shed on Italian soil? None. No, Brutus, what I did was a Right Act. Zeno would see that, even if Cato did not. I chose to honor the idea of Roma when her laws had gone astray.

BRUTUS
But that way lies destruction, don't you see? Caesar, the gods have gifted you with a mind that sees the

rationality of your argument - you can't imagine not seeing the reasonable chain that brought you to your opinion, link by link. But someday there will come lesser men, men not so gifted, who will not follow your excellent reasoning. They see only the results. One man, acting outside the law without fear of consequence. One man, ruling a mighty empire. One man, become a god. I will say this for Sulla - he stepped down, relinquished his grip, gave it up voluntarily when his work was done.

CAESAR
That's the third time you've mentioned retirement. Do I detect a hint?

BRUTUS
A plea, rather. Tomorrow, in the Senate, announce you're stepping down as Dictator. Go to your war, by all means. But as a proconsular general.

CAESAR
*(laughing)* And be forced to do it all again? Dear dear Brutus, soul of Rome, who knows these men so well, tell me - after I have dipped below the horizon, how long would it be before some enterprising senator offers a bill condemning my actions? Oh, something minor at first, no teeth to it. A vote to recall my exiles. That always sounds good, makes for more votes. Then another bill, invalidating one of my laws, perhaps on religious grounds. Inarguable. Then another, a little more pointed. Suddenly we're at the races, each senator driving his chariot pell-mell towards condemning me at law. Hearings, investigations, public outcry. All at once I'm in Parthia, fighting a war on two fronts - the foreign foe before me, my country-

men with daggers at my neck. I'll win the first war only to find myself – again! – with no tool at hand to balance the scales but my army. *(beat)* Come, Praetor Urbanus. You've heard the evidence. Sit in judgement of your Dictator. Is Caesar guilty of any crime, save loving his country?

BRUTUS
The businessmen could not be allowed to profit from their crime, you said. They had to leave the company. Follow your own sentence.

CAESAR
You think I enjoy absolute power?

BRUTUS
If you love your country, step down.

CAESAR
Brutus, be practical. I cannot.

BRUTUS
Cannot is not the same as will not.

CAESAR
My will is not in question.

*Enter ANTONY, a drink in his hand. He's thirty-nine years old, extremely fit – broad-shouldered and well-muscled.*

ANTONY
Here you are! Damn, uncle, are you still working? Leave off, enjoy yourself for once. Brutus, you ninny, you were supposed to bring him back, not turn into his clerk.

CAESAR
Antonius, we have different ideas of pleasure, you and I.

**ANTONY**
Do we? Not as far as women are concerned. It'll take me another ten years to I rack up as many feminine corpses in my wake. Even at your age, you're like a siege machine. Bam bam bam! Well, I happen to have a stout battering ram of my own. Ha! *(quaffs his cup, then points at the carafe next to BRUTUS)* Is that wine?

**CAESAR**
Help yourself.

*ANTONY crosses and pours. He notices the map on the desk.*

**ANTONY**
Oh-ho! I take it all back. Is this the plan for Parthia?

**CAESAR**
It is.

**ANTONY**
Ex-cell-ent. Eight legions - you always go in undermanned. But I suppose the local kings will fall over themselves to give you troops. Why let Romans die when there are perfectly good foreigners to take the arrows for them, right?

**CAESAR**
Just so.

**ANTONY**
*(throwing himself into a chair)* Just like old times. *(to BRUTUS)* Except this time we're not fighting you and your friends. Not that you did any fighting. Did you even draw your sword? No no, no shame in it. You're not a killer.

**BRUTUS**
Whereas you are.

**ANTONY**
A lady-killer. Are we planning a stop in Alexandria on the way?

**CAESAR**
It's as good a port as any. Why?

**ANTONY**
I hear Aegypt is fabulously wealthy.

**CAESAR**
I think the queen might object to us looting her country.

**ANTONY**
Then shut her up with your battering ram. Bam bam bam! *(laughs)* Seriously, Caesar, why not take what's yours? You married her. Makes you a kind of king. Caesar Rex. So the treasures of Aegypt belong to you.

**CAESAR**
Your logic is faulty. I'm married to Calphurnia, not Cleopatra.

**ANTONY**
I heard you married--

**CAESAR**
After their custom, not a Roman wedding.

**ANTONY**
Pity. You could have covered up your sparse top with a decent crown.

**CAESAR**
*(to BRUTUS)* How would you like to be going bald

when your very name means 'thick head of hair?' *(to ANTONY)* For the record, Antonius, Caesar has no interest in Cleopatra's crown - or *anyone else's*.

ANTONY
Alright, alright! Jupiter. Suppose I should be grateful. If your marriage was legal, Cleopatra's son would be your heir, not me. Thank the gods Calphurnia's barren! *(drinks)* Is the queen still in Rome? I've been meaning to meet her, but my wife's afraid I'll fall under her spell the way old Caesar Rex has!

CAESAR
'Old Caesar Rex.' Antonius, you are seldom as funny as you think you are, and drink only heightens your self-amusement.

ANTONY
'And drink only heightens your self-amusement.' Who talks like that, honestly? You're like someone out of Homer.

CAESAR
Whereas you've stumbled out of a Satyr play.

ANTONY
*(toasting CAESAR)* I take that as a compliment.

CAESAR
I knew you would. *(to BRUTUS)* The maddening part is that he can be so capable. You'd never know it to look at him, Brutus, but when he sets his mind to it, my nephew can pile Pelion on top of Ossa. Sadly he loves pleasure more than duty.

ANTONY
Don't lecture me, uncle. I'm not a child anymore.

**CAESAR**
No. Children can be taught.

*There is a heavy silence.*

**ANTONY**
Oh, before I forget. Brutus - Cassius is looking for you. *(grins at BRUTUS, then shifts his gaze to CAESAR)* You missed a great debate in there.

**CAESAR**
Oh?

**ANTONY**
I posed a deep philosophical question. 'What is the best way to die?'

*BRUTUS blanches, stares.*

**CAESAR**
An ill-omened subject. Typical Antonius. And what were the answers?

**ANTONY**
Cassius said, 'On the battlefield, sword in hand.' That fool Lepidus said the best death was sheer old age, surrounded by children. Trebonius' answer was funny. He said, 'Free.'

**CAESAR**
And you, Antonius? What is your ideal death?

**ANTONY**
In a good fight. By which I mean, for love or money.

**CAESAR**
And with a mouth full of wine, no doubt.

**ANTONY**
Absolutely! And my siege machine up some girl's

*cunnus.* Ha! That's the way to go! *(no one else is laughing, so he pulls a face)* So, what's your answer, uncle?

CAESAR
That some of us don't have time to play idiot games. There's a war on the horizon.

ANTONY
You know what you should do, Caesar?

CAESAR
Tell me, Antonius. I am all agog.

ANTONY
Give the Parthian war to me. I'll go and conquer for you, in your name. You keep hammering your wives, hammering the Senate too. I know you love work - writing laws and such. You're good at it. And you've had so many great wars - leave something for us poor younger men to do!

CAESAR
Is that what I should do?

ANTONY
Absolutely. Don't worry, I'll stick to your plans. The victory will be in your name. Caesar will still be the hero. I'll be the drudge, do all the work, while you relax here and have your fill of fun.

CAESAR
A most generous offer, Antonius. Wouldn't you say, Brutus?

BRUTUS
I say we left out a third kind of Roman earlier. Pragmatist, Dreamer - and Cynic.

CAESAR
*(laughing)* Just so. Antonius, it is kind of you to offer to spare these old bones the trials of another war. But as I said, you and I have different notions of pleasure. A bottomless flagon of wine and an endless sea of breasts do not appeal to me the way they do to you. So why don't you stay in Rome, and Caesar will conquer for himself.

ANTONY
If Caesar doesn't care for breasts, he can have a sea of young boy's backsides instead. Just like old King Nicomides did for you. That little pansy Octavius can be first--

*CAESAR is around the table like lighting, hauling ANTONY out of his seat and gripping his throat in one hand. ANTONY tries to break CAESAR's grip. To his surprise, he can't.*

BRUTUS
Caesar--

*CAESAR continues choking ANTONY. Outside, the storm rages.*

BRUTUS
*(frightened by CAESAR, yet trying to be reasonable)*
Caesar, he's drunk. *(beat)* You're in Lepidus' house. *(bravely)* Think of your *dignitas*.

*CAESAR continues a moment more, then releases his hold. ANTONY falls to his knees, gasping.*

CAESAR
Get out of my sight. But first thank Brutus for your life, Antony. And be in the Senate tomorrow morning, on time and sober. I have an announcement I

want you to hear firsthand.

*ANTONY stalks to the door, rubbing his throat.*

ANTONY
I'll be there, Caesar.

*With a significant look to BRUTUS, ANTONY exits.*

CAESAR
*(shaking)* No. *(sits down)* Water, Brutus.

*BRUTUS quickly pours CAESAR some water.*

BRUTUS
Should I fetch a--

CAESAR
*(drinking deeply)* No. No no. I'll be fine. *(drinks again)* These fits. I never had them before Aegypt. Why is that? And why do I get them most when Antony is involved?

BRUTUS
What a brute.

CAESAR
Apt. He should carry your name.

BRUTUS
The first Brutus got that title by feigning boorish behavior. Antony's the real thing. Are you well?

CAESAR
*(drinking again, more calmly)* My fault. My fault. As I get older, I find my temper lives far closer to the surface. Maybe that's what brings them on - anger. Nobody can make me angry like Antonius. Imagine that drunken excrement calling me a bumboy. If he were anyone else - family is a wretched nuisance!

**BRUTUS**
I know.

**CAESAR**
Thankfully, there is a surprise in store for our friend Antony.

**BRUTUS**
You'll announce tomorrow that he's not going to the war?

**CAESAR**
More than that. I'll read my will. No one will have any doubt of my intentions.

**BRUTUS**
You're serious? He's not your heir?

**CAESAR**
A useful brute he may be, but he'll never be up to the task. I've chosen an heir with more political sense in his little finger than Antony has his his whole body.

**BRUTUS**
Octavian. It's your nephew Caius Octavius, isn't it?

**CAESAR**
You are the most perspicacious man I know. Between us, yes, I'm adopting young Caius Octavius as my heir.

**BRUTUS**
And you expect Caesar's heir to be able to enter the Senate as just another senator.

**CAESAR**
He's too young to enter the Senate for at least another ten years. His only possible route is the

one I took, an act of bravery on the battlefield. But he's no more a natural military man than you are. So he'll have to wait, and by the time he's old enough, awe of me will have faded.

BRUTUS
Provided you're not still alive.

CAESAR
Don't worry. I won't be.

BRUTUS
*(sharply)* What do you mean?

CAESAR
Those whom the gods love best are never permitted a full span of years. Besides, I've always disliked the idea of dying - I'd much prefer to be killed. Though at times like this, I think it will be my temper that kills me. All I ask is these next five years. Having conquered the West, I'll take the East, and the whole world will be Roman!

BRUTUS
Five years!

CAESAR
And even then, Brutus, even then there's so much to do! Laws in desperate need of passing. Reforms and contingencies. Public works - sewers, roads, replacing brick with marble in the temples. A dedicated body of public fire-fighters, working for the state to protect rich and poor alike. Tell me - if I were not Dictator, riding herd over them, would the Senate ever pass such necessary laws?

BRUTUS
It's possible.

CAESAR
But likely?

BRUTUS
No.

CAESAR
Exactly. The Senate is interested in itself only, and even that interest is short-sighted.

BRUTUS
So you advocate a perpetual dictatorship.

CAESAR
Quite the contrary. My task is to set up laws that are so comprehensive, so utterly fair and detailed, that there will be no need ever again for someone to take the road I've been forced to walk. There must be no dictator after me.

BRUTUS
If you do not step down, there will be. I guarantee you. Step down and there's hope.

CAESAR
No, you are wrong. It must be by my death.

BRUTUS
If you do not give up the power, the Republic will die.

CAESAR
The Republic is an idea, and like all ideas it dies only if not cherished.

BRUTUS
You sound like Cato.

CAESAR
Hmph! I suppose I do. We should have been allies,

your uncle and I. But Cato saw compromise as defeat. Even when we agreed on policy, he took the opposite side. If I was for it, it had to be wrong.

BRUTUS
You did sleep with his wife.

CAESAR
*(shrugging)* He was my political enemy. He's the one who made it personal.

BRUTUS
Ha! Only Caesar... *(going from amused to tentative)* Caesar, I - I understand his last earthly act was to write to you.

CAESAR
Alas, no. Cato's last earthly act was violence upon himself. I was the penultimate issue for him.

BRUTUS
How did he die? My wife won't tell me.

CAESAR
Like the good lady Portia, my intention has always been to spare you suffering. Suffice to say, he died like he did everything - hard, and chin up.

BRUTUS
Can you at least tell me what he wrote you?

CAESAR
*(laughing sourly)* Typical Cato. He pointed out that I had no legal right to pardon people, and he refused to be pardoned by someone acting illegally.

BRUTUS
*(laughing too)* Perfect Cato. He was right, of course.

**CAESAR**
Brutus, more than any other man--

**BRUTUS**
I know. It was Cato who forced you to cross the Rubicon. Unwavering, unmoving. My wife is still proud of him.

**CAESAR**
As a child should be of her father. As I hope my adopted son will be of me one day.

**BRUTUS**
Caesar - about Octavius. There are rumors--

**CAESAR**
Yes. Antony mentioned them in his usual, tactful way. Have no fear. The lad and I have had that particular conversation.

**BRUTUS**
That bad?

**CAESAR**
Better than I'd hoped. I put it off for months. But before he left for Brundisium I told him to stop his adoring looks at Agrippa. The problem is the boy's so pretty - save for those ridiculous ears. I don't think he's actually attracted to men. But the slur will always be present for him. So I gave him the same advice my mother gave me.

**BRUTUS**
Your mother discussed it with you?

**CAESAR**
I had no one else. Like you, I grew up fatherless. Come to think of it, we are both products of our mothers. Yours coddled. Mine did not.

**BRUTUS**
Coddled. Not a word I would have used.

**CAESAR**
I suppose not. Servilia is unique. I think she's always waited for you to stand up to her. She used to tell me--

**BRUTUS**
What advice did your mother give you?

**CAESAR**
Ah, yes. After the rumor about Nicomides started spreading, mother said if my affairs were secret, everyone would assume I was sleeping with men. So my affairs had to be public. Not unmarried girls, just the wives of prominent men. *(chuckling)* It became a habit.

**BRUTUS**
I know.

*CAESAR looks at BRUTUS sharply, then tries to defuse the moment by laughing.*

**CAESAR**
How open I am tonight! Truly a evening of candid conversing.

**BRUTUS**
You're a piece of work.

**CAESAR**
How so?

**BRUTUS**
Even your adultery is based on rational arguments. Your passion is thought-out, like a battle plan.

**CAESAR**
Women and war - two sides of the same coin.

**BRUTUS**
*(brutally)* Did you cuckold Lepidus as well?

**CAESAR**
What?

**BRUTUS**
I met our host's daughter at the door and almost dropped dead of shock.

**CAESAR**
*(wistfully)* Yes… I often come here just to drink in the sight of her. Aemelia is a gift from the gods. For I swear, as more years go by, I have trouble recalling my daughter's face.

**BRUTUS**
How is that possible? There was more promise in Julia's smile than in all the sunrises in the world.

**CAESAR**
I miss her too.

**BRUTUS**
So, is Aemelia your--?

**CAESAR**
I only cuckold my enemies. No, Lepidus has a share of Julian blood, and Julian girls are always fair.

**BRUTUS**
I know. Look at my sister.

**CAESAR**
*(surprised)* Ah. Do you wish to have that conversation? Truly?

**BRUTUS**
I don't know. Yes. When will I have the chance again?

**CAESAR**
Not for five years, at least. But some things are best left unsaid.

*CAESAR stands, pours BRUTUS a drink.*

**CAESAR**
Are you happy with your wife?

**BRUTUS**
*(taking the offered drink, sips)* She's - passionate.

**CAESAR**
I didn't mind, you know.

**BRUTUS**
What?

**CAESAR**
You marrying her.

**BRUTUS**
Why should you?

**CAESAR**
*(archly)* Now who's pretending an ignorance he doesn't own? A man I pardon for fighting against me marries the daughter of my most implacable foe? Hmmm. A lesser man might see that as an insult. Even a challenge.

**BRUTUS**
Thank the gods you're not a lesser man. *(drinks)* When did it begin? You and mother. When did it start? Exactly.

**CAESAR**
Just after I met her. She fascinated me. Reminded me of my mother. Another woman who should have been a man.

**BRUTUS**
When?

**CAESAR**
Some years after your father died. She came to me to propose that you marry Julia. Why?

**BRUTUS**
*(holding the cup in two hands)* Oh.

**CAESAR**
Oh! Oh, no, Brutus! Jupiter! I'd heard the rumors too, but I never never thought you would *believe* them!

**BRUTUS**
But my little sister, Cassius' wife, she's..?

**CAESAR**
My daughter, yes. Though I've never met her, and do not know her.

**BRUTUS**
Cassius - I think that's part of the reason he married her. To be your unofficial son-in-law. And since she's so clearly your daughter, I thought perhaps...

**CAESAR**
No, Brutus, no. If you had a glass, you would see there's not a drop of Caesar in you. You are a true Junius Brutus, the son of your father, descended from the first Brutus, the man who overthrew the last king of Rome and founded the Republic.

**BRUTUS**
While you are descended from those kings.

**CAESAR**
I prefer to think of Aeneas and Romulus - and Venus. But not you. No. Poor Brutus. How long have you--?

**BRUTUS**
Ever since I found out. About you and mother.

**CAESAR**
I never intended that to come out.

**BRUTUS**
I know. That was mother's fault. One of her rare mistakes.

**CAESAR**
Yes, sending love letters during a heated Senate debate is hardly discreet.

**BRUTUS**
I wonder if she did it to force you to marry her.

**CAESAR**
If so, she misjudged me. I would never marry a woman who had been unfaithful to her husband.

**BRUTUS**
Even if it was you she was unfaithful with?

**CAESAR**
Caesar's wife must be above suspicion. I refuse to have any flawed thing in my life.

**BRUTUS**
Again - perfection. *(smiles wanly)* But the fact that she has flaws will be news to her.

**CAESAR**
A remarkable woman, your mother.

**BRUTUS**
Neither of her husbands were your political enemies.

**CAESAR**
Servilia is a case apart.

**BRUTUS**
Do you love her? Did you ever?

**CAESAR**
*(laughing sharply)* That harpy? No. *(beat)* I apologize. You deserve a real answer. No, I did not love your mother. But she interested me. She has a mind. Like your wife, she is passionate. She is also scrupulous about her status. Her affair with me notwithstanding, do these gossips actually think she would have given her honor to a fourteen year-old, no matter how august his birth?

**BRUTUS**
She *did* give her honor to you.

**CAESAR**
Not until I was man enough for her. But even if they believe--

**BRUTUS**
Go ahead, say it. Even if *I* believe.

**CAESAR**
Very well. Even if you believe that she would have given herself to a pubescent boy, do you honestly think I would have let you espouse my daughter if you were my son?

**BRUTUS**
Incest doesn't seem to bother you.

**CAESAR**
That's changing horses in the middle of the race.

**BRUTUS**
I think it's spot on topic.

**CAESAR**
There is no question of incest. Cleopatra will have no more children by me.

**BRUTUS**
How can you be sure?

**CAESAR**
I am sure. That is enough.

**BRUTUS**
As I understand their ways, your son can only be Pharaoh if he marries his full sister.

**CAESAR**
Then he will not be Pharaoh. Aegypt's Queen will bear me no more children. But you're mistaken. These things have happened quite often in the past - a child is born with no full sibling. So the mother takes a lover who bears some of the father's blood. A brother, a cousin. Perhaps I should introduce her to Octavius. They're almost of an age.

**BRUTUS**
You're not serious.

**CAESAR**
Of course not. I just own a perverse sense of humor. Octavius is horrified by her. Though I think he's really just jealous of the time I spend with her.

### BRUTUS

He's not alone. Half of the Senate goes to that woman's house hoping to find you there. I imagine Calphurnia wonders where you are at night.

### CAESAR

Calphurnia is the most excellent of women, and Caesar's true and faithful wife. I'm leaving her everything I legally can. Even if, as seems likely, Calphurnia has no child, she will be well-provided for. One-eighth of my fortune to her, another eighth to various relations - *not* Antonius. There are bequests for those public works I mentioned. The rest goes to Octavius.

### BRUTUS

*(hearing very little of this)* You're not my father.

### CAESAR

Dear dear boy. No. Would I could claim such an honor. If I had a Roman son--

### BRUTUS

Please, no.

### CAESAR

You don't seem pleased. You thought - you thought I broke off your engagement to Julia because of a blood tie between you two. Oh Brutus, no. I needed Pompey, so I bound him to me with the strongest tie I had - my daughter. Which meant breaking her engagement to you. I regretted it then, and now. But needs must. *(smiling ruefully)* Pompey was never my ideal son-in-law.

### BRUTUS

Is that why you killed him?

CAESAR
*(stung)* I did not kill him.

BRUTUS
Had him killed. The Greeks say that's as good as doing the deed yourself.

CAESAR
Greeks say a lot of things. Brutus, I had nothing at all to do with Pompey's death. That was Cleopatra's brother. It's what made me side with her in the first place. I wanted nothing more than Pompey alive and well and living in Rome again, battling me in the Senate instead of the field of Mars.

BRUTUS
*Your* Rome. *Your* Senate.

CAESAR
A Rome where a man may get his due.

BRUTUS
Who's to say what is his due? Today that right belongs solely to the Dictator.

CAESAR
Are we talking about the Senate, or Julia?

BRUTUS
We're talking about Caesar the King, Caesar Rex! Caesar the undisputed genius, the great man, conqueror, lover, politician, poet. Alexander, Theseus, Socrates, and Homer all rolled into one. The first among equals, *primus inter pares*! Caesar the god!

CAESAR
I am none of those things. I am a man. And your friend.

**BRUTUS**
My friend, yes! That's the part I can't - I want to hate you, Caesar! For my mother, my uncle, my wife, for my self - for Roma! But you *are* my friend. The only person who ever understood me.

**CAESAR**
Except Julia.

**BRUTUS**
Don't! I - don't! *(stands and moves away from CAESAR)*

**CAESAR**
I told you. Some things are best left unsaid. *(beat)* Beware the Ides of March.

**BRUTUS**
The Ides are tomorrow.

**CAESAR**
I'm well aware of it.

*Thunder.*

**BRUTUS**
It's funny, isn't it. You can see everyone else so clearly. But you can't see yourself through our eyes. Do you know how much you've changed our world? Do you have an inkling what your existence has done to Roman life?

**CAESAR**
*Do I know?* Half a million people made homeless, by Caesar. Four hundred thousand women and children dead, on Caesar's orders. A hundred thousand men with severed hands, at Caesar's command. A million enemy soldiers slain, by Caesar's armies. A million more men, women, and children sold into slavery, to line Caesar's

pockets. The sacred boundary of Roma crossed by Caesar's army. By Caesar. All done in Caesar's name, for Caesar's honor - for Roma. *(beat)* My only consolation is knowing I always tried the path of law before the path of blood. And when I have destroyed, what I have left behind shall benefit future generations in far greater measure than what I was forced to destroy. Do you imagine, Brutus, I don't see the sum total of the devastation and upheaval I've caused? Do you think I don't grieve? Do you think that I don't look back on it - and forward to more of it - without sorrow? Without pain? Without regret? You mistake me, Brutus. Thank the gods, I won't live to be an old man. I don't think I could bear it.

*CAESAR seems more vulnerable in that moment than BRUTUS has ever seen him - slumped shoulders, head down. He looks, above all else, tired. BRUTUS reaches out a hand, pulls it back, then makes a decision.*

BRUTUS
Caesar--

*Huge thunder - the storm has grown into a tempest. A window blows open. Papers on the desk scatter.*

CAESAR
*Cacat!* Brutus - help!

*CAESAR closes the shutters again while BRUTUS gathers up the papers.*

CAESAR
Thank you. Quite a tempest!

BRUTUS
There's a fiercer one in my head. *(notices the paper in*

*his hand)* What's this map?

CAESAR
That? Oh, it's nothing. I'm expanding Rome's borders. Well past time, I think.

BRUTUS
Expanding Romulus' realm. And that's nothing. Regal benevolence. Godlike, even.

CAESAR
Do you truly not approve, or are you simply angry at me? Never let emotion cloud your sense, Brutus.

BRUTUS
*(setting the map down)* I'm sorry. I got sidetracked by - by personal issues. You're right. Better left unspoken. Let's be reasonable about this.

CAESAR
By all means. Do you have a suggestion?

BRUTUS
I'm not talking about the map. Caesar, you cannot remain Dictator. I see the sense in all your arguments. You want to build a new Rome - a reasonable, ordered Rome. But you don't see that the foundations you're laying are made of sand. *(laughing bitterly)* You know the real problem? We love you.

CAESAR
*(amused)* Yes, I can see how that--

BRUTUS
All of Rome admires and adores you, the man. You always have the right words, you have humor and gravitas in equal parts. You're brave and sure and smart - and honest! You're always honest! You've brought order, you've righted wrongs, you've passed

fair and just laws for men of all classes. Rome loves you. And that's more dangerous than anything. Because we love you, we turns a blind eye to all you represent. *We're* the real problem here. *We're* the ones willing to let you forge ahead. *We're* the ones giving you power. If we simply refused to consent, your power would vanish. If you're an adder, we're the ones giving you the stinger.

CAESAR
An adder's sting? Not even a lion's tooth, or a leopard's claw?

BRUTUS
You do have the luck of a giant cat.

CAESAR
Caesar's luck will be proverbial.

BRUTUS
Caesar's luck. Not my luck, Caesar's. When you talk that way, it's royalty speaking. The royal *we*. Caesar, tell me truly - and please, a straight answer - do you wish to be made king?

CAESAR
Never. Never, Brutus. Absolutely not. *(BRUTUS is relieved until CAESAR goes on)* After all, what is king? Rex is a word. Caesar is a word. Why would I want to be called King? To be Caesar is better than being king. I want no honors, no trappings, and certainly no crown. But-- You, Brutus. You.

*Thunder.*

CAESAR
You of all men might understand. Seven civil wars in my lifetime. Seven. Add to that proscriptions,

purges, and outright murder, and what do you have? Chaos. Rome is foundering. You must see that. Our customs and beliefs are dashing themselves against the facts of our times. The ideals of our founders are either ill-equipped for modern man, or else ill-served by him. The poor are frightened by the change, and they cling to the three staples of their lives - their gods, their games, and their bread. The Second and Third Classes want to join the First Class while the First Class wants to protect its exclusivity. We with the birth, the money, and the will to govern are expected - needed - to provide for the lesser among us. Else the Republic will fall.

BRUTUS
The Republic is eternal.

CAESAR
Nothing is eternal. Not even the gods. Without a firm hand, we will return to Pandora's world - a world of chaos. It's almost as though someone has defied the gods and shouted out Roma's secret name into the open air, heralding our destruction.

BRUTUS
Is that the choice? Caesar, or chaos?

CAESAR
Not a palatable choice, I'll confess. But you must see that a dictator is better than destruction.

BRUTUS
I'm not so sure. We cannot have a king - or a Caesar - and still be the people our forefathers envisioned.

CAESAR
But they couldn't envision the state in which we find ourselves today! We're no longer that tiny

colony on the seven hills, desperate to survive the wolves. We have interests in foreign lands, far-flung peoples and places. Our wealth is great, our prestige greater, our enemies greater still. The sign-posts our ancestors planted should guide us to who we will become, not bind us to who we were. An example - from the time of our founding until a generation ago, the poor had no stake in the society. The army was filled with men of means - men with property have property to defend. But that changed when Marius saw Rome's need for soldiers - an honest need, with the Germans coming for us like an avalanche. Lacking men, he drafted the poor. Practical. But fifty years on, what do we have? Professional soldiers coming home to find themselves rejoining the poor, wondering why they were called to fight for their country. Was it to join the Head Count and starve once discharged? Military training married to starvation births revolution. And not one of our civil civil wars, with Senators battling Senators. This will be a genuine uprising, with the people overthrowing the lot of us. As a consequence, Rome today needs wars, constant wars, foreign wars, until we are prosperous and equitable here at home. Without wars abroad, we sow the seeds of our own destruction.

BRUTUS
Perpetual warfare? That's a terrible solution!

CAESAR
Offer an alternative. Should we tax businesses? The poor? Women? That is the choice - wars of conquest, or taxation. War is both popular and profitable. We can try to replace it with arena

games, but nothing matches the patriotic fervor of war, nor its ability to produce funds.

BRUTUS
We should just return to the old ways. Leave the rest of the world to fight each other. Remain above it.

CAESAR
We tried! We tried, but they came for us anyway! Carthage, Pontus, the Germans - we fought them and fought them until we saw the only way to keep them at bay was to conquer them. I am not saying I approve, Brutus. I'm saying this is where we are.

BRUTUS
Are we a nation of brigands, then? Foreign wars are theft writ large.

CAESAR
Whereas civil wars are not about wealth or land. They're about our idea of ourselves. Most men are sadly incapable of defining themselves by what they are, so they rely on what they are not. Being Roman has to mean more than merely not being Greek or Aegyptian. If we cannot have a foreign foe to define us, we will create one within our own ranks. And the sides will forever line up between youth and learning on the one hand and tradition and dogged ignorance on the other. One side sees the need for change, while the other sees the passing of the old ways and resists.

BRUTUS
No illusion to which side you favor in that struggle.

CAESAR
There is value to our history, but it cannot dictate our future.

**BRUTUS**
Says the Dictator.

**CAESAR**
Says Caesar. I never wanted any of this. It's terrible to look around and realize one has no equal. The men who might have given me a run for my money – Clodius, Cato, Crassus, Pompey – they're all dead. I'm like the Lighthouse of Alexandria. Nothing stands half so tall. It's not the way I wanted it, but Caesar had no choice.

**BRUTUS**
No choice!

**CAESAR**
Roma needs a strong hand. A man with vision enough, foresight enough, to create a framework for the future. You of all people should understand that. It was the first Brutus who created the frame that serves us to this day.

**BRUTUS**
By killing a king.

**CAESAR**
Any man can murder. No, your namesake did something far grander. After he deposed the Tarquin, the people offered Brutus a crown. And he refused. *He refused.* Do you realize how astonishing that is? Such a bold act of self-denial, of patriotism! It leaves me breathless. The greatest deed in our history, the founding of the Republic, the bedrock upon which we have built our world – the notion that we can rule ourselves.

**BRUTUS**
Yes! Exactly! We can rule ourselves!

CAESAR
But now it's five hundred years later and his Republic is gasping, tired and old. We need another Brutus, another man of sense to reset Rome's foundations for another five hundred years.

BRUTUS
You.

*Thunder.*

CAESAR
Who else? Honestly, Brutus, who else? I don't relish the job. But I love my country. What was I supposed to do? Sit and watch while fools like your uncle and his friends cling to tradition so tightly that they squeeze away our future?

BRUTUS
You couldn't have, even if you wanted to. You're a born autocrat. And that is why we're afraid.

CAESAR
We?

BRUTUS
You have the blood. Descended from Venus and Romulus, you said. If ever Rome was to have a king again, it would be you. And Rome cannot have a king.

CAESAR
I agree. Rome cannot have a king, the people would never stomach the word. *The word.* But if there is a man with the power of a king but without that title - *that* they could tolerate. That they could even embrace. Because the people are not blind.

They know that government isn't working – or if it is, not in their interest. If, to right a litany of injustices, to set Roma back on her feet, to again make her the city on a hill – if to do that I have to take the power of a king, I will.

BRUTUS
Caesar Rex.

CAESAR
Rex is a word. I am Caesar. To be Caesar is far greater than to be king.

BRUTUS
That first Brutus – he murdered his own sons so that they could not be hailed as kings after him. Would you?

CAESAR
A moot point. I have no sons.

BRUTUS
Caesarion.

CAESAR
*(dismissively)* Cleopatra's son will sit on the throne of Aegypt, never in Rome's Senate.

BRUTUS
Octavius, then. You said yourself, he is your heir.

CAESAR
Does that trouble you? It is easily remedied.

*CAESAR takes up a sheet of parchment and writes upon it.*

CAESAR
'I, Caius Julius Caesar, Imperator and Dictator Perpetuous, being descended from Venus through

her son Aeneas, and from Romulus the founder of Rome, do hereby adopt as my son and heir Marcus Junius Brutus, descendant of that first Brutus who founded the Republic. I do this in all good conscience and free from duress. Long Live Rome.' Care to witness? Just your name, Brutus. I'll lodge it with the Vestals tonight and the thing will be done.

BRUTUS
*(horrified)* No! No, absolutely not. It – it would not be a Right Act.

CAESAR
Are you certain? If not you, Brutus, then the choice must fall on young Octavius.

BRUTUS
Let it fall on his head, then. I can think of no worse fate than being named your heir.

CAESAR
That – is quite a statement.

*Both fall silent. Rain lashes at the windows. CAESAR crosses and pours himself a cup of wine. BRUTUS places his head in his hands. CAESAR notices.*

CAESAR
Brutus, are you well? Shall I call for someone?

BRUTUS
I feel – very alive.

CAESAR
What?

BRUTUS
Caesar – Antony's question? What's your answer?

CAESAR
I haven't decided to die yet. What is your answer?

BRUTUS
That depends. Am I talking to my friend Caius Julius, or to Caesar the god?

CAESAR
Your friend, always.

BRUTUS
Then I say the best death is in a good cause.

CAESAR
Would a man ever die for a bad one? That is a cheat, my boy.

BRUTUS
Better than not answering.

CAESAR
Oh Brutus! What does the manner of death matter, so long as it's quick?

*There is a knock on the door.*

SERVANT
Caesar, pardon me. Marcus Brutus, your brother Cassius asked me to fetch you to him. He was most insistent--

CAESAR
*(setting down his cup)* We are both on our way. Come, Brutus. We must crush a cup of wine and drink to the Ides - for I believe they are upon us.

BRUTUS
I'll be right there.

*CAESAR exits, followed by the SERVANT.*

*BRUTUS paces. Outside the window, the storm grows wild. Finally BRUTUS pauses, looking out at the tempestuous sky.*

BRUTUS
Caesar, or Chaos.

*BRUTUS crosses to the table, where the will CAESAR just wrote is sitting. He picks it up and reads it over, feelingly. Then he downs a cup of wine.*

BRUTUS
It must be by his death.

*Thunder. A series of lightning flashes strike through the room. Each flash is a projection of images of CAESAR's assassination. There are classical paintings, statues, and coins, all portraying the death of CAESAR. Amid the swelling thunder voices become clear, shouting:*

VOICES *(V.O.)*
Liberty! Freedom! Tyranny is dead!
Run hence, proclaim, cry it about the streets.
Some to the common pulpits and cry out
"Liberty, freedom, and enfranchisement."

*BRUTUS holds the piece of paper close to his heart.*

BRUTUS
*Sic, semper tyrannis.*

## BLACKOUT

## END OF ACT ONE

# II

OCTOBER 2, 42 BC

# Act Two

### Phillipi
### A Military Tent - Dusk

*A table sits at the mouth a large military tent, with camp chairs. BRUTUS is seated at the table looking down on a map, shuffling pieces around aimlessly. He appears preoccupied, mind elsewhere.*

*Seated in a chair overlooking the camp is MARCUS TERENTIUS VARRO, seventy-four years old. Writing furiously, he suddenly looks up.*

VARRO
It's tomorrow?

BRUTUS
So Cassius thinks. Mark Antony's men are down there in the marshes, trying to build a ramp.

VARRO
*(making a note)* Tomorrow is Cassius' birthday.

BRUTUS
I heard. Young Cicero thinks a fine present would be Antony's head on a spear.

**VARRO**
Without a tongue, no doubt. I miss his father. Poor Cicero. He was like me - unwarlike in the extreme. Whereas his son is a true *virs militaris*, a born soldier.

**BRUTUS**
*(aside)* I wish I were.

**VARRO**
Have you noticed, Marcus Junius, that fathers are seldom blessed with the sons they deserve?

**BRUTUS**
'Few sons are like their fathers-- most are worse, few better.' Homer.

**VARRO**
Brave Scaurus had a coward for a son - shit himself on the battlefield. Horrid old Sulla's son was an absolute sweetheart. He died, of course. Cato's father was a gentleman, and Cato was - well, Cato.

**BRUTUS**
They say that greatness skips a generation. My father was a great man.

**VARRO**
Your father was briefly great because your mother pushed him to it. When he failed to heed her advice, he ran afoul of Pompey and was killed.

**BRUTUS**
I always forget you were there. Marcus Terentius Varro, the eternal biographer, witness of all the catastrophes of Rome. No wonder the gods brought you to Philippi.

**VARRO**
Not the gods, Marcus Junius. Antony. My property, my wealth, all gone. What else could I do?

**BRUTUS**
Cross the Rubicon.

**VARRO**
What did I ever do? I fought for Pompey, yes – he was my friend, what else could I do? But Caesar pardoned me. He was a bastard, but fair – always gave a man a second chance.

**BRUTUS**
A mistake Antony does not mean to repeat.

**VARRO**
What did I ever do? I write books.

**BRUTUS**
He's afraid of the one you'd write about him.

**VARRO**
He should be afraid of the one I'll write about you.

**BRUTUS**
No point. If I die tomorrow, there's no one left to carry on my name. The Junius Brutus line stops here.

**VARRO**
You should adopt someone.

**BRUTUS**
What, and leave a death sentence as my bequest? Better the name dies with me. Brutus once meant noble regicide. Thanks to Antony and Octavian, it now means traitor. Betrayer. Murderer.

**VARRO**
Liberator.

**BRUTUS**
Perhaps you can make it so. But it will take a mighty pen to restore my name. My legacy is ruined. In trying to honor my ancestors, I've blackened their names, and mine.

**VARRO**
Brutus, Brutus! You make it sound as though we've lost already! We have all the food. If we can hold out, Antony and Octavian will starve.

**BRUTUS**
Their men may. Antony feeds on hate. And I don't think Octavian eats at all.

**VARRO**
*(laughs darkly)* Octavian! What a final joke! If Caesar was Theseus, his life-thread fraying all those around him, Octavian is Odysseus, manipulating everyone to his own ends. Just twenty-one, and somehow he's made himself equal to Antony. Consul! Puny little nothing that he is. Down in Hades, Caesar's shade must be laughing himself sick to see us run from the viper he dropped in our midst.

**BRUTUS**
He's not in Hades.

**VARRO**
What?

**BRUTUS**
Nothing. Did Caesar have it right, do you think? Is it better to choose your heir?

**VARRO**
Well, one cannot choose one's bloodline. So yes, adoption is the strongest way to gain the heir one desires. Like I said, the children of great men often prove disappointing to their fathers.

**BRUTUS**
Mothers too.

**VARRO**
And how is the lady Servilia?

**BRUTUS**
She'll outlive us all.

**VARRO**
I did hear an odd story. That when she heard Caesar was dead, and at your hand, she ran down to the market and began shouting out the secret name of Rome.

**BRUTUS**
Completely true. She felt it was better Rome should end then, at that moment, than... *(shrugs)* We got her back into the house and shut her up. I have scars from her claws.

**VARRO**
Ha!

**BRUTUS**
Too late. Roma's secret name was spoken aloud. The contract with the gods was broken.

**VARRO**
If you believe in such things. Curses and prophecies...

**BRUTUS**
And ghosts.

**VARRO**
She hasn't forgiven you?

*BRUTUS is silent.*

**VARRO**
It must be hard, torn between her two great loves - you and Caesar.

**BRUTUS**
As it turns out, not hard at all.

**VARRO**
*(probing)* I was sorry to hear about your wife.

**BRUTUS**
Thank you. Her brother is over in Cassius' camp.

**VARRO**
Another disappointing son. It's not in him. Your Portia would have been a far better son to Cato. As it was, she died a daughter who would have made her father proud.

**BRUTUS**
What do you -- is that how Cato died? Choking on--?

**VARRO**
What, don't you know?

**BRUTUS**
No one would ever tell me.

**VARRO**
Cato took a knife and opened his belly. He then sat reading Plato until he passed out.

**BRUTUS**
That's not so--

**VARRO**
*(holding up a hand)* Young Cato found him, got the doctors to him in time to sew him up and revive him. When Cato saw he was still alive, he howled, tore open his stitches, reached inside himself, and threw his guts across the room.

*BRUTUS looks like he might gag.*

**VARRO**
A determined man, even when it came to death.

**BRUTUS**
Like he did everything. Hard, and chin up. *(shakes himself)* Forgive me, Marcus Terentius. The night before a battle, and here I am talking old family gossip. I have dispositions to see to.

**VARRO**
*(rising)* You should get some sleep.

**BRUTUS**
Time enough to sleep tomorrow.

**VARRO**
*(from the tent flap)* Good night, Brutus.

**BRUTUS**
*(making a show of being busy with the pieces on the map)* Good night.

*Once VARRO is gone, BRUTUS steps away from the map and surreptitiously draws out a letter. He looks it over.*

**BRUTUS**
Bitch.

*CAESAR enters, not from the tent's flap, but from the shadowy corner of the tent.*

**CAESAR**
What's the disposition of the troops?

**BRUTUS**
*(hiding the letter)* Their placement, or their mood? Sour, both. I think that--

*BRUTUS stills, then slowly turns.*

**BRUTUS**
So. You return.

**CAESAR**
As promised.

*BRUTUS is shaking, his heart racing - he's terrified.*

**BRUTUS**
What-- *(steeling himself)* What do you want?

**CAESAR**
*(briskly)* Tell me how matters stand.

**BRUTUS**
*(without taking his eyes off CAESAR)* Antony and Octavius are down there in the marshes, waiting to avenge you. We're about equal in numbers, but we've stripped the land of food. They're already suffering. Cassius says they'll attack tomorrow to keep from starving. *(beat)* Are you here to help them?

**CAESAR**
I'm here for you.

*CAESAR advances. BRUTUS quickly retreats, walking backwards and keeping the map table between them.*

**BRUTUS**
Stay back!

*CAESAR ceases to advance. Enter VARRO at the run.*

**VARRO**
Brutus! Are you-? What is it?

*VARRO is standing scant feet away from CAESAR, but obviously doesn't see him. BRUTUS stares back and forth between them, tempted to ask.*

**BRUTUS**
Nothing. I - dozed off. I dreamed of Caesar.

**VARRO**
Typical of the man. Always the conqueror, invades even our dreams. Get some rest.

*VARRO turns to leave.*

**BRUTUS**
*(eyes on CAESAR)* Varro - stay close.

*Nodding, VARRO exits.*

**CAESAR**
*(crossing to peer out the flap of the tent)* Oh, I've missed this! The night before a great battle, how it fires the blood. Makes one feel alive!

**BRUTUS**
That would be a miracle.

**CAESAR**
*(wryly)* Indeed. *(crossing to the table with its pieces representing legions.)* I see you've let Cassius run things. Probably wise. But why on earth did you agree to make two separate camps?

**BRUTUS**
The hill has two peaks.

**CAESAR**
Too much, I suppose, to take a page from my book and circumvallate the whole hill. Well well, what's done cannot be mended. *(starts moving pieces)* What you must do now is draw them up into an attack on the marsh side. That fool Antony will be proud of his ramp, and commit too many of his men to defending it.

*Hands shaking, BRUTUS draws his dagger, and approaching CAESAR's exposed back.*

**CAESAR**
Then, while he's slogging around, you must punch through Octavian's line and take their camp. They won't expect you to come down off your perch and act. Boldness, Brutus, boldness will save the day. *(without turning)* Strike, or sit. Your trouble ever was lingering on the precipice of action.

**BRUTUS**
A failing I overcame.

**CAESAR**
True. *(steps away from the map, where he's created a winning strategy)* There! I still have the knack. How very helpful I am, advising you how to defeat my avengers.

**BRUTUS**
I find your advice a little suspect. I'm not even sure I believe you're real.

**CAESAR**
Yet here I am - waiting to be invited to sit.

*Unnerved, BRUTUS lays his weapon on a table and gestures vaguely at a camp stool. CAESAR sits, but restlessly, tapping his fingers and bouncing his foot.*

BRUTUS
You're more talkative than last time.

CAESAR
It takes some getting used to, this – condition. I hope you do not see volubility as a failing. I have so little conversation nowadays.

BRUTUS
You're truly a ghost?

CAESAR
Shade, please. Or spirit. Present company excepted, I don't go around haunting people.

BRUTUS
*(momentarily amused, in spite of himself)* A ghost with a taste for sophistry. Sorry, shade. Are you solid?

CAESAR
Let's find out. Try stabbing me again.

BRUTUS
Am I supposed to apologize?

CAESAR
I'm not here for an apology.

BRUTUS
You won't credit this, but I've missed you. Really missed you.

CAESAR
I believe you, Brutus. If only because I haven't been here to extricate you from your usual muddle!

**BRUTUS**
*(ruefully)* Octavius. That was some trap you laid.

**CAESAR**
Yes, my nephew will go far.

**BRUTUS**
He's calling himself Caesar now.

**CAESAR**
Why not? I adopted him.

**BRUTUS**
Not Caesar Octavianus. Just Caesar.

**CAESAR**
Probably pleases his men.

**BRUTUS**
Whereas mine tremble and quake. I see now I should have accepted your offer.

**CAESAR**
You didn't want to diminish your name.

**BRUTUS**
I didn't want to be accused of profiting by your death. It had to appear noble.

**CAESAR**
It could hardly appear otherwise. You are Brutus.

**BRUTUS**
Brutus. Brutus the liberator. Brutus the betrayer. Am I the villain of your story, Caesar, or are you the villain of mine?

**CAESAR**
Each man is the hero of his own story. The rest is for men like Varro.

*Unable to sit any longer, CAESAR stands and begins to move about the tent, looking at this or that.*

BRUTUS
Cassius was against coming here, giving battle. He wanted to give ground, make them chase us, the way Pompey did to you. He preferred Fabian tactics, starving Antony and Octavian out.

CAESAR
A tried and true strategy. Pompey only lost when he dared to face me.

BRUTUS
I was in Pompey's army. I saw what constantly retreating did to the men. They were terrified of that battle long before it took place. No, I've decided to put my fate into the hands of the gods. Rome's future, on a single battle. If we win, I am vindicated. If we lose… What was it you said when you crossed the Rubicon? 'The die is cast.'

CAESAR
That's not what I said.

BRUTUS
No?

CAESAR
Far too fatalistic. 'The die is cast.' I was quoting Menander. *Anerriphtho kubos*. 'Let the dice fly high!' I embrace risk.

BRUTUS
While I resign myself to fate. I want this over. What the Ides of March started, tomorrow will finish. End. Complete. *(beat)* What is death like?

CAESAR
Restless. Frustrating. Above all, surprising. I never subscribed to an Underworld or Elysium. I expected, if not peace, then a vast nothingness. I believed that the end of life was the end of existence.

BRUTUS
Apparently you were mistaken.

CAESAR
Apparently. What about you?

BRUTUS
What about me?

CAESAR
Was my death what you thought it would be?

BRUTUS
---No.

CAESAR
You thought that with me dead, everything would return to what they used to be. Back to normal. The scales balanced.

*BRUTUS nods.*

CAESAR
And now it's chaos.

BRUTUS
You warned me as much. But then you always had the power to foresee consequences. Can you still? Can you tell me what will happen tomorrow?

CAESAR
*(whispering portentiously)* There will be a battle. Men will die.

BRUTUS
*(sourly)* Very helpful.

CAESAR *spreads his hands apologetically.*

BRUTUS
Can you see the outcome? The fate of Rome?

CAESAR
Rome? Rome will endure, Rome will fall, only to rise again in another nation, another age. Rome is an ideal, Brutus. You know that better than any man. Rome will endure as long as men have the will to die for an idea.

BRUTUS
What idea?

CAESAR
You tell me. It was for that idea that I was sacrificed.

BRUTUS
Sacrificed?

CAESAR
*Sacre fice* - to make holy. I understand I'm now a god of the Roman pantheon. I'm fairly certain I don't approve.

BRUTUS
You were worshipped in life. You're surprised that death made you a martyr? *(sotto voce)* People keep dying.

CAESAR
*(darkly amused)* Did you think my death would end all earthly cares? Death gives life meaning. Without it, we would all be gods and our existence would be a series of pointless bickerings and liasons.

**BRUTUS**
Aren't they that already? *(irritably)* Can't you sit down?

**CAESAR**
Forgive me. I am - rest less.

**BRUTUS**
Do you visit anyone else? Dole out vague warnings and expert military advice?

**CAESAR**
No one else has need of me.

**BRUTUS**
Need of you? I thought you were here to murder me. My evil spirit.

**CAESAR**
Perhaps I am. The villain of your life, you said.

**BRUTUS**
My wife is dead.

**CAESAR**
---I'm sorry.

**BRUTUS**
I have a letter here. From my mother.

**CAESAR**
I can't imagine she broke the news kindly.

**BRUTUS**
*(laughing)* No. Not kindly at all. She says that Portia had been growing frantic ever since I came East. When no one was looking, she swallowed hot coals.

**CAESAR**
Shades of Crassus! Brutus--

**BRUTUS**
It isn't true. It can't be true. When the Parthians poured molten gold down Crassus' throat, they used a special device - a tube, wasn't it?

**CAESAR**
Yes.

**BRUTUS**
Because the human body can't swallow fire. Physically, it can't. No, I know what happened. She knows my fears. An airless death... Unable to punish me directly for killing you, my loving mother forced those burning coals down Portia's throat.

**CAESAR**
That sounds - just like Servilia.

**BRUTUS**
My fault. Unintended consequences. I don't think I loved her. I married her in some feeble show of defiance. I exepcted you to lash out. But it was my mother who made me pay. We live in horrible times. *(considers)* Is that true? Or are the times always horrible, and I've just never noticed?

**CAESAR**
Men are men. We are capable of great beauty. But it is far easier to destroy.

**BRUTUS**
I'm not out to destroy anything! I thought I was putting things right! *(puts his head in his hands)* Such a fool. They were all lying. Cassius, Trebonius, Casca - said it was for honor, for the Republic. Lies.

**CAESAR**
Politics.

**BRUTUS**
Cicero's brother - he published a pamphlet on getting elected, advising candidates to promise lavishly, promise anything to anyone. Far better to break a promise, he said, than to tell them the truth from the start. A very successful political strategy, as it turns out. Such a fool! 'We must restore the Republic,' they said. I listened to their words, never hearing their greed, their envy, their anger. Did you die for revenge? For personal gain? Did we strike down the greatest man in the world for something so petty as money?

**CAESAR**
Do motives matter?

**BRUTUS**
Of course motives matter! Motive is the heart of--

**CAESAR**
A man on trial can justify his actions, prove his motives were pure. But no matter what he says, the deed exists.

**BRUTUS**
You always justified your actions.

**CAESAR**
Which didn't change them. Just made them easier to live with.

**BRUTUS**
Maybe that's their comfort - they can say they did it for liberty and justice. But somehow I'm not comforted.

**CAESAR**
You are honest.

**BRUTUS**
Does that doom me? Must I die for honesty?

**CAESAR**
That depends on if Truth is worth dying for.

**BRUTUS**
In the abstract, of course, yes. But when faced with it...

**CAESAR**
Death is not an abstraction. Death is very real.

**BRUTUS**
I don't want to die with my work unfinished.

**CAESAR**
When you die, your work is finished.

**BRUTUS**
If that's true, why are you here? Isn't this unfinished business? Why are you here?!

*CAESAR is silent for a moment. Then he picks up a book.*

**CAESAR**
Cicero? What is this?

**BRUTUS**
A gift from young Marcus. All his father's speeches against Antony after - after the Ides. He called them his Philipics--

**CAESAR**
After Demosthenes. Amusing. Philipics at Philipi. *(sighs)* Poor Cicero. So scared, yet so clever. That golden tongue of his was both gift and curse - he always let it run away with him.

**BRUTUS**
Antony cut out that golden tongue. And the hands that wrote those words. Free speech is dead. *(shaking his head)* When did it go wrong? Can you tell me? When did that happen? Was it cheap bread to the masses? Was it the provinces? The standing armies? When did we lose our way? When did we stop being the people we claim to be, want to be - believe ourselves to be?

**CAESAR**
You know my answer.

**BRUTUS**
When we stopped believing in the Law.

**CAESAR**
A legal system only works so long as all men agree to it. When those charged with making the laws hold them in contempt, it is chaos. I saw it coming, so I acted.

**BRUTUS**
And in so doing, broke the law.

**CAESAR**
If motives matter, condemn my deed, but not the motive.

**BRUTUS**
You said once that Rome is the deeds of Romans. I condemned you for fighting injustice with more injustice. You crossed a river. I murdered a man. How am I different?

**CAESAR**
You did as your honor demanded.

**BRUTUS**
My honor! None of the others thought of their honor. And the worst part? They were right! I should have killed Antony. Probably Octavian and Lepidus too. If I'd been just a little more practical, we might not be here tonight.

**CAESAR**
You are a dreamer.

**BRUTUS**
Brutus' Dream.

**CAESAR**
You saw the cynics and practical men as you saw yourself.

**BRUTUS**
Did I? Or was I just eager to cloak my deeds in their words? They wanted you dead for envy, jealousy, revenge. Were my motives any better?

**CAESAR**
Do motives matter?

**BRUTUS**
When I struck I wasn't thinking of honor or kings or my great ancestor. The gods forgive me, I was thinking of my mother, of my sister, of the humiliation. Of your arrogance, pardoning men as though you were a god already. I was thinking of all the hundred wrongs you'd done me through my life. The wreckage my life had become. All because of you.

**CAESAR**
You were thinking of Julia.

**BRUTUS**
That, above all! You're the one famous for clemency, Caesar. Not me! I don't forgive you, not for that! You stole her--

**CAESAR**
Brutus, she never--

**BRUTUS**
She could have learned to love me!

*CAESAR advances towards BRUTUS, hand outstretched. BRUTUS recoils.*

**BRUTUS**
Stay back!

*CAESAR stills. BRUTUS weeps.*

**CAESAR**
She could have, yes. She was the perfect Roman woman. She knew her duty towards her husband. But you would never have known if she loved you for you, or because I told her to.

*BRUTUS sags.*

**CAESAR**
I had no idea how much you hated me. It seems so clear now. When I crossed the Rubicon, you joined with Pompey, the very man who not only killed your father, but also married your great love. I thought you did it because you believed in the cause. Now I see it was personal.

**BRUTUS**
Everything is personal.

**CAESAR**
Would it comfort you to know that my death was

not the cause of this war?

BRUTUS
What?

CAESAR
Rather I should say, this war would have happened regardless. Alive or dead, there would have been war. Antony's ambition is too great. Had I lived, he would have risen against me. Perhaps you would have joined him. Cassius, certainly. When the battles were done, they would have turned on each other. The result is the same.

BRUTUS
It's not the same. I'm not the same. It doesn't matter about the war - I mean, it does, but-- I'm different. Me. I murdered a man. Not just any man, but the greatest Roman that ever lived.

CAESAR
Brutus--

BRUTUS
Let's not fool ourselves. You tower over Rome like a god. Cassius called you a Colossus, with the rest of us peeping out from between your feet. You're a once in a lifetime mind - a hundred lifetimes. A Wonder of the World.

CAESAR
The Colossus of Rhodes fell. Feet of clay.

BRUTUS
Oh, you were flawed, Caesar. But that doesn't change who you were. You say the war would have come anyway. Is that supposed to be a comfort? If that's true, then our actions are meaningless. That

means this stain on my soul is pointless. *(beat)* I'm so tired. Is endurance really a virtue? *(with a half-smile)* I wonder, will my shade come back to haunt Antony in his final hour?

CAESAR
You don't love Antony.

BRUTUS
Are you saying you love me?

CAESAR
As much as I love Roma herself.

BRUTUS
And isn't that a glowing testament of affection! Civil war, the government shattered, countless lives ruined! Oh, please, Caesar, do not love Rome so dear. Rome cannot endue any more of your love. Nor can I. Go. Leave me, spirit.

CAESAR
As you wish.

*CAESAR starts to exit.*

BRUTUS
*(startled)* That's it? I say go and you go?

*CAESAR is silent.*

BRUTUS
Will I see you again?

CAESAR
This is the last time we shall speak, you and I.

BRUTUS
Not quite what I asked. *(beat)* I understand, now.

How it felt. Crossing the Rubicon.

CAESAR
Yes, I imagine it was much the same. Steeling your will to what must be done, while--

BRUTUS
While regretting the necessity. *(touches his breast)* I felt what you were talking about. That broken piece inside. Such a little thing, taking a life. And yet monumental. A greater crime by far than crossing a river.

CAESAR
A death is a death, be it the death of a man or a death of a dream.

BRUTUS
Brutus' Dream. That's certainly dead. In the space of a single generation, we've wrecked it.

CAESAR
*(sardonically)* Well, we did have help... Perhaps we shattered the Republic. But, Brutus, as we sit here in the horrendous aftermath of our lives, you must admit that it was cracked and leaking before we came along.

BRUTUS
My life is not over!

CAESAR
Of course not. Not until you are finished with it.

*BRUTUS looks sharply at CAESAR.*

BRUTUS
Now we come to it. That's why you're here. You

know what I'm thinking - you always know.

CAESAR
I may have misjudged your thoughts once or twice.

BRUTUS
*(unwilling to be diverted)* Ending a life - so simple, so huge. Antony's question on the eve of the Ides. I didn't have an answer then. I still don't. How does Brutus die?

CAESAR
If you win tomorrow, you shall die an old man, surrounded by friends, just the way Lepidus wished for us all.

BRUTUS
Pretty to think so. I have an ill-divining spirit. If, as seems likely, we lose, what do I do? Run, like Pompey did? No. I'm not such a coward. How does Brutus die? Go to Rome in chains and be thrown from the Tarpean Rock? Die like Cato, hard and chin up?

CAESAR
You see why I spared you that tale.

BRUTUS
Protecting me was never your job. You are not my father.

CAESAR
You approve, then, of Cato's death?

BRUTUS
I'm as horrified as I am disgusted. Zeno calls suicide a Right Act. A man's ultimate power, choosing to end one's own life. But it seems wrong.

CAESAR
So don't do it. Find a stout enemy sword and die upon it instead. Nothing simpler.

BRUTUS
That's no better! Tantamount to the same thing, only it puts my death on another man's soul. Oh, how does a Brutus die?

CAESAR
What does it matter, so long as it's quick.

BRUTUS
It matters, Caesar. If not to the dead, then certainly it does to the living. Your death turned you into a martyr.

CAESAR
A martyr to what?

BRUTUS
I had hoped, to democracy. To the Republic. But it didn't turn out that way.

CAESAR
No. Because you failed to heed your own advice. Democracy cannot be imposed. That's as true for Brutus as it is for Caesar. True democracy starts at the heart of a society - with the Plebs, the common man. Why do you think I tried so hard to provide for them?

BRUTUS
To gain their love.

CAESAR
*Post hoc, ergo propter hoc.* No, Brutus. I worked for them because if they are prosperous, so is Roma.

Neglecting them is doom – something the Senate forgets to their peril. I provided for the Plebs to preserve Rome. That they loved me for it was gratifying, but was not the cause.

BRUTUS
They burned down half of Rome with your funeral. By murdering you at the height of your power, I gave you immortality. If the gods struck men dead with irony, we'd be shades together. I doubt I'll be made a god after my death. You were a god among men. I, a man among gods.

CAESAR
Apt. I never sought worship, you know. Merely respect. Those who can should be allowed to do.

BRUTUS
Now who's the dreamer? In what world did you live? Men's egos are as fragile as Aegyptian glass. You shattered men's pride, seduced their wives, upended their laws, defeated their armies. You expected to win their forgiveness too?

CAESAR
Theirs? I suppose not.

BRUTUS
What am I doing? You're not even here. The night before the battle, and I've lost my wits--

CAESAR
You are not mad, Brutus. For all our fury, we are not mad.

BRUTUS
Fury?

**CAESAR**
We are pursued, you and I, by the Furies. The Kindly Ones. The gods' revenge for killing those we love.

**BRUTUS**
If you've come to kill me, do it! No matter who wins tomorrow, Rome cannot survive. Like you, too many blows have been struck to its heart.

**CAESAR**
I wish you weren't so determined to condemn yourself. It makes for tedious conversation. And this from someone starved for talk.

**BRUTUS**
Don't you see other shades?

**CAESAR**
From time to time. But I've not been able to speak to them. They open their mouths, sometimes, and I hear - something. It's very like music. But no words, no thoughts. If I address them, they simply shake their heads and move on.

**BRUTUS**
Something to look forward to.

**CAESAR**
I am not used to such indifference. Anonymity is not for me. Better reviled than forgotten.

**BRUTUS**
So you would have taken the crown.

**CAESAR**
I told you, Rex is a word. To be myself was far more than king. King is a title little men give themselves to show their power. Poor Gnaeus Pompeius was the embodiment of what I speak.

**BRUTUS**
Pompey never called himself king. He wouldn't have dared.

**CAESAR**
Indeed not! But what was his name? Gnaeus Pompeius *Magnus*. The Great. A name given to himself, by himself. So deeply insecure, his own name would never suffice. Instead, like a child dressed in an adult's toga, he gave himself a magnificent title. But there are names that ring out down the ages louder than Rex or Magnus. Pericles. Alexander. Hannibal. Achilles. Hector.

**BRUTUS**
Caesar.

**CAESAR**
Brutus. For us all, the name is enough.

**BRUTUS**
What about those that follow, then? The ones who'll never meet you, never know you. Those hollow men who will wrap themselves in your name and leave ruin in their wake.

**CAESAR**
You do not know.

**BRUTUS**
But I do! This night of all nights, I see things clearly. You were right, motives matter less than deeds! Whatever my motives, my deed will be remembered! I will be a beacon of light, a warning that will ring down the ages - Sic, semper tyrannus. Thus tyrants must fall. I did right! You hear me? *I did right!*

**CAESAR**
I never said you did not.

*BRUTUS is about to speak when he's interrupted by a shout from offstage.*

**VARRO**
Brutus! Brutus!

*Enter VARRO, running as fast as he is able, a smile on his face. He comes up short, looking around - he does not see CAESAR.*

**VARRO**
Were you talking--?

**BRUTUS**
*(glancing CAESAR's way)* I was - rehearsing my oration to the troops.

**VARRO**
*(excitedly)* You may not need it! Antony has come, under a flag of truce!

*BRUTUS turns to CAESAR, who smiles wanly and opens his hands.*

**CAESAR**
Perhaps all is saved.

**BRUTUS**
Should I receive him?

| **CAESAR** | **VARRO** |
| I would. | A general must. |

**BRUTUS**
*(nodding)* Very well. Send him in.

**VARRO**
Do you want me-?

**BRUTUS**
No, this is not a meeting for history. The results will speak for themselves.

*Disappointed, VARRO exits. BRUTUS turns to CAESAR.*

**BRUTUS**
What will he want?

**CAESAR**
To win.

*Enter ANTONY. He is dressed in full military regalia. He stops sharply and gives a proper salute.*

**ANTONY**
*Salve*, Marcus Junius Brutus.

**BRUTUS**
*(saluting in kind) Salve*, Marcus Antonius.

*ANTONY relaxes.*

**ANTONY**
Got any wine?

**CAESAR**
Nothing changes.

**BRUTUS**
Over there by the tent flap. Help yourself.

**ANTONY**
*(crossing to pour)* Thank the gods you're civilized. I remember the old warhorse never let me drink on campaign. And they say he was a great man. Feh. *(drinks)*

**CAESAR**
Old warhorse.

**ANTONY**
*(looking about him)* Nice. A little Spartan for my taste, but still, a proper commander's tent. Must be nice to have money. *(throws back the rest of the wine, starts pouring again)* Heard about your wife. I'd say I'm sorry, but I'd be lying. She was one of the plagues you left behind you in Rome.

**BRUTUS**
Explain yourself.

**ANTONY**
Oh don't get all peevish! I was talking about the women - all of them! You hear what they did? All those noble ladies - your wife, Cicero's old battle-axe, that barren cunt Calphurnia, even your harpy of a mother! Never thought anything would bring all those women together. But there they were, marching in lockstep like a proper legion!

**BRUTUS**
Why?

**ANTONY**
Why else? Money! We needed it! Lepidus and Octavius and I, we needed gold to come chasing after you, more gold than we could get from confiscating your lands and property. So we had the Senate decree a tax on women.

**BRUTUS**
You're joking.

**CAESAR**
*(laughing)* Fools. Never wake the women.

ANTONY
Can you imagine it? All those widows with fat allowances, living in their villas on the Palatine and Aventine. They could fund a war against Olympus! But would the crafty bitches pay? No! You know what they did? Put on their husbands' armor and marched into the street. A legion of women, beating swords on shields and breastplates screaming, 'No voice, no money! Give us our voices and we'll give you our gold!' Can you believe it? They wanted the vote!! Said if they were going to be taxed, they ought to have a say in government!

CAESAR
Good for you, Calphurnia.

BRUTUS
And what did you do? Send in your armies?

ANTONY
What could we do? That's one law that was revoked in record time. Let the gorgons keep their gold. *(clapping his hands together)* So, Marcus Junius, I imagine you can guess why I'm here.

BRUTUS
To surrender?

ANTONY
Ha! Funny! Never knew you to joke. But seriously, you have to give up. It's the only honorable thing to do.

CAESAR
Honorable.

*CAESAR moves ANTONY's wine goblet to his other side.*

BRUTUS
This, from you. You promised you wouldn't speak against us. An amnesty.

ANTONY
You promised Caesar loyalty. An oath is only as good as circumstance allow. And I didn't speak against you - kept my word to the letter. Besides, be fair, when I made the promise I thought I was Caesar's heir. Then I read the will. That snake Octavius...

BRUTUS
Don't like your partner?

ANTONY
*(rolling his eyes)* He's not - I don't know - *(spits)* Can't even talk about him. At least you have a colleague you can work with. Cassius, that's a real man. Married to your sister to boot. Family.

BRUTUS
Octavius is a cousin of yours, isn't he?

ANTONY
No, now he's Caesar's son. Young Caesar! Caesar reborn! *Cacat! Mentula!* No no - not a man! He's as cunning as a woman! *Verpa! Fellator!*

*ANTONY reaches for his drink, finds it missing, then discovers it on his other side. Puzzled, he drinks.*

BRUTUS
*(looking at CAESAR, supressing a smile)* Family is a wretched nuisance.

*CAESAR winks.*

**BRUTUS**
So, did you come here to complain? I'm afraid you haven't chosen a very sympathetic ear.

**ANTONY**
*(setting his drink down again)* No no. I came because you're a man of sense. Thank you for making two camps. I could never have had this conversation with Cassius present. Jupiter, I doubt I'd leave this room alive if he were here.

*BRUTUS looks to CAESAR, who has just moved ANTONY's drink again. ANTONY traces his gaze and glances around uneasily.*

**ANTONY**
He's not, is he?

**BRUTUS**
No. We are quite alone, you and I.

**ANTONY**
Good. Listen, Brutus, let's be men and end this. Why spill more Roman blood? If you surrender, Cassius'll have no choice but do the same. You'll be a hero.

**BRUTUS**
I've been a hero. It doesn't last.

**ANTONY**
Well, that's true enough, isn't it? There's always a new darling for the mobs around the corner. It amazes me Caesar lasted as long as he did. But then he always had the luck.

*ANTONY reaches for his cup, which has moved again.*

**BRUTUS**
Luck? Give the man his due, Antony. He made his

luck.

ANTONY
*(finding his drink)* Hmph. Surprised to hear you of all men defending him.

BRUTUS
You shouldn't be. So, what are you offering?

ANTONY
The lives of your men, and Cassius' men.

BRUTUS
A noble offer. And for myself and Cassius? The other Liberators?

ANTONY
I'd like to offer safe passage to Rome and a fair trial. But young Caesar has taken an oath to see you dead. I can't promise he won't murder you the moment you hand over your sword. He's learned from Caesar's clemency. Leave no enemy alive. *(grins)* You see why I couldn't bring this offer to Cassius.

BRUTUS
Whereas you think I relish the prospect of dying?

ANTONY
Cassius will do anything to survive. You do what you believe is right. Brutus is an honorable man.

*BRUTUS favors ANTONY with a stoney glare. ANTONY smirks back. He's decided to keep his cup in his hands.*

BRUTUS
Antonius, your army is starving. We have the high ground and more supplies. And if I'm not a natural military man, neither is Octavius. Matched for men,

and with those advantages, why would I consider surrender?

ANTONY
To end the war.

CAESAR
*(to ANTONY)* And do so on your terms, giving you a victory over Octavius as well. Oh very good, Antony! It's almost clever. You'll look like the peacemaker, the clement one - picking up the sole piece of my legacy young Octavian has spurned. *(to BRUTUS)* Ask him what will happen to your soldiers?

BRUTUS
What will happen to my men?

ANTONY
I'll take personal charge of them. They'll have to swear allegiance to me, become my clients. Small price to guarantee their lives.

CAESAR
And providing Antony a personal army to wage war against Octavian when the time comes. Clever, clever Antony.

BRUTUS
What will you use them for?

ANTONY
I mean to finish what Caesar started - the war against the Parthians. He laid it all out, no reason those splendid plans should go to waste. I'll keep moving East, honor the old boy's memory.

CAESAR
Ruinously expensive.

BRUTUS
With what money?

ANTONY
Oh, I plan to stop by Aegypt first. Still haven't met the queen. She must be in mourning. I'll ask her to donate some of her vast wealth to complete Caesar's last wish.

BRUTUS
And if she refuses?

ANTONY
I'll take what I need.

CAESAR
Making you richer than Octavius. You'll return from the East a hero and have yourself named Dictator. Clever, clever Antony. *(to BRUTUS)* Turns out all he needed was a spur.

ANTONY
Well?

BRUTUS
How long do I have to decide?

ANTONY
How long do you need? To a patriot, the answer should be obvious. End the war, even if it means giving your life for your men.

BRUTUS
Admit that I was wrong.

ANTONY
I can promise you a better death than the one you gave Caesar. *Ecastor*, I'll even let you fall on your sword! Can't be fairer than that! It's more than

Octavian'll give you.

CAESAR
What does it matter, so long as it's quick?

BRUTUS
Wait a moment. How do you know what kind of death we gave Caesar? You weren't there - you were outside, with Trebonius.

CAESAR
Yes. Trebonius.

ANTONY
There were plenty of witnesses. I heard--

BRUTUS
Trebonius - Trebonius.

ANTONY
What about him?

BRUTUS
After the murder, he was genuinely astonished you'd run away. He seemed-- *(beat)* Antony, the night before the Ides, at dinner, you asked a question.

ANTONY
*(pouring himself a fresh cup)* Did I? I don't remember. Had a lot to drink that night.

BRUTUS
You asked what was the best way to die.

ANTONY
*(quaffs his drink at one pull)* That's right, I did. What about it?

BRUTUS
You bastard. You knew. You and Trebonius, you had

a side arrangement, didn't you? Fixed it up between you. When I spoke out against killing you alongside Caesar, Trebonius was the only one who took my side. He told you what we were planning, didn't he? If things went bad, you were supposed to get him off. After all, *he* didn't stab Caesar - he was outside, with you! Only you betrayed him. You ran, and came back playing the role of the heir, all outraged innocence. He was stuck playing his part. You bastard.

ANTONY
I shook your hand. I kept my word. I said nothing against you to the people.

BRUTUS
You're a bastard, Antony. A demagogue, a sot, and a, a--

CAESAR
Betrayer.

BRUTUS
Yes, a betrayer.

ANTONY
That's rich! Brutus calls me betrayer! That's being called tall by a giant. Your betrayal dwarfs mine, oh honorable one. If mine even existed. And as Trebonius was the first Liberator to die, there's no way to prove anything.

BRUTUS
You and Octavian deserve each other. Oh, how I wish I'd been there when you heard the will! I knew, by the way. Caesar told me. He even offered--

ANTONY
What?

*BRUTUS crosses to a locked box. Opening it, he produces a piece of paper, carefully preserved. Contemptuously he hands it to Antony, who reads it over.*

BRUTUS
The night before the Ides, he offered to make me his heir. Anyone but you, he said.

*For a moment ANTONY is still, his face contorted in rage. He makes to tear the paper, but BRUTUS snatches it back. ANTONY pauses, then shakes himself, throws back the last contents of his cup.*

ANTONY
You have until dawn, Brutus. Think of your men. Think of your honor. Think what Caesar would do.

CAESAR and BRUTUS
Caesar would destroy you.

ANTONY
Well, that's not something I have to worry about, is it? Thanks to you.

*Giving BRUTUS a mock salute, ANTONY exits.*

BRUTUS
That must've stung.

CAESAR
I saw him for what he is. He's clever like a hammer's clever.

BRUTUS
A drunken hammer, hitting nails askew at random.

CAESAR
Bam bam bam.

*They start to laugh.*

**BRUTUS**
Is that bulge for real?

**CAESAR**
I'd say he stuffs his loincloth, but I've seen him. All his brains are between his legs!

**BRUTUS**
The man is an utter, absolute, irredeemable ass.

**CAESAR**
King Midas got his ears from Antony.

**BRUTUS**
And such a letch! Whenever I think of him, I imagine a rutting beast nosing up some waif's skirt!

**CAESAR**
And a trough of wine.

**BRUTUS**
I know! Does he have a third leg? Where does all the wine go?

**CAESAR**
*Veni, vidi, vomui.* He came, he saw, he vomited!

*They fall about laughing.*

**BRUTUS**
*(laughter subsiding)* Is his offer real?

**CAESAR**
I imagine so. Not because he honors his word. He needs those men. Octavian has all my clients and most of my soldiers. And he has my personal wealth.

**BRUTUS**
From what I hear, the army refused to march if he wasn't with them. They think he's lucky.

CAESAR
Well, he is - he's Caesar's heir! But like you told Antony, a man makes his own luck.

BRUTUS
Which doesn't help me in the least. Now I've another choice to make - thank you, Antonius! Die, and save my men. Or fight, and watch them fall.

CAESAR
You were lamenting a lack of choices. As these things go, this isn't a poor one. Your life for that of your men.

BRUTUS
An admission of guilt.

CAESAR
No. Of defeat. Victory doesn't always go to the one in the right. Sometimes circumstance, not justice, decides a war.

BRUTUS
If I hand them over, they'll just die in the next war.

CAESAR
That's not on your conscience. A man is responsible for his choices, not those of others.

BRUTUS
If I give in to save my men, what does that say about the lives already lost?

CAESAR
The dead are past caring. Worry about the living.

BRUTUS
You're here. Are you past caring?

**CAESAR**
So you'd throw good Roman lives after dead ones? Sisyphisian, the last dead man justifies the next one. Where does it end?

**BRUTUS**
If they die in a just cause...

**CAESAR**
What does it matter if the cause is just, if it is lost?

**BRUTUS**
Motives matter.

**CAESAR**
Results matter more. History will not judge the quality of the cause, only the number of men lost.

**BRUTUS**
No. History forgets the men. There are always more men. It's the cause that lingers. Some things worth dying for. *(beat)* Does it hurt?

**CAESAR**
I cannot answer the general. Only my own experience. Yes. It hurt. Then it didn't.

**BRUTUS**
You died well.

**CAESAR**
I had Pompey's example. I saw his statue and remembered - they said he hid his face so that his murderers could not see it. What's the line from Homer? 'In his death all things appear beautiful.'

**BRUTUS**
Which brings us back to the question. How does Brutus die?

CAESAR
Ignore motive. Look at the deed.

BRUTUS
The deed. If I surrender to save my men, history will record I didn't believe in my side enough to fight. If your death taught me anything, it's that how a man dies matters - if not to him, to posterity. *(beat)* I have to try. Even if it's a lost cause, I can't just submit, not when there's a even a gossamer-thin chance. That's not the way a Roman behaves. We may fall, we never surrender.

CAESAR
So good men must die to hold up your image of yourself.

BRUTUS
Let the dice fly high. Don't think I don't see the irony. But I'm willing to go a step further than you... *(struck by a thought)* That's it. That's the answer, isn't it?

CAESAR
What is?

BRUTUS
Murderers should not profit from their crime.

CAESAR
Go on.

BRUTUS
Law. Justice. Force, counter-force. Order, chaos.

CAESAR
Speak plainly, Brutus.

**BRUTUS**
It's not that you were wrong to cross the Rubicon. You were balancing an injustice. But by not stepping down afterwards, by trying to impose order on Rome, you created your own injustice. Which I ended. It ends with me. *(with realization)* It must be by my death.

**CAESAR**
Brutus, what are you--?

**BRUTUS**
You fought against the tyranny of the nobility. I fought against the tyranny of Caesar Dictator. Thus, always tyranny. You were justified to cross the Rubicon. I was justified to kill you for it. Force, counter-force. Both were Right Acts. And with my death, I'll save Rome again.

**CAESAR**
How? Make me understand.

**BRUTUS**
Chaos is the weapon of the gods. In trying to impose order, we were agents of chaos. Because chaos isn't only the best weapon of the gods - it's their greatest gift! It's freedom. Freedom is infinitely harder than tyranny, and infinitely preferable.

**CAESAR**
Softly, Brutus. Take me with you.

**BRUTUS**
One cannot uphold the law by breaking it. Yes, if the law is itself broken, we must act. But that's not enough! Endurance *is* a virtue. If breaking the law is necessary, we must also uphold it by embrac-

ing the consequences. That's what never happens. Caesar broke the law, then held himself above the consequences. Brutus broke the law. To mend it, Brutus must accept his fate.

CAESAR
Return to Rome and face trial?

BRUTUS
If that were an option. You heard Antony. I would never reach Rome - your heir would see to that. Either I must win and go to Rome to submit myself for a trial, or else die here a free man.

CAESAR
By your own hand?

BRUTUS
*(steeling himself)* If need be. What greater act of freedom can a life have than choosing to end it? *(with conviction)* It must be by my death. Just as Caesar had to pay the price of his illegal acts, so must Brutus. *(turning to CAESAR)* I'm right, aren't I?

CAESAR
Who am I to say? I am only Caesar. You are Brutus.

BRUTUS
I will fight tomorrow. If we lose, I will die as well as you did. Chin up, like Cato. I will accept the consequences of my actions. *That's* how Brutus dies.

*A glow creeps in - the sun is beginning to rise. Looking at it, BRUTUS starts chuckling.*

CAESAR
Is something amusing?

**BRUTUS**
I'm sorry, it's just – I was afraid you'd come to kill me. Instead Caesar's ghost has helped me decide how to end my life. I'm relieved. No more muddle. I see clearly now. A fitting revenge.

**CAESAR**
That is not why I came.

**BRUTUS**
*(surprised)* No?

**CAESAR**
You kept my will.

**BRUTUS**
*(picking up the will)* I didn't mean to show it to anyone.

**CAESAR**
I am here because of that. I am here because your mother shouted out the secret name of Rome. I am here because of my one regret.

**BRUTUS**
And that is?

**CAESAR**
I regret you were not my son.

**BRUTUS**
*(astonished)* What?

**CAESAR**
When I broke your engagement to Julia, I wounded you far more deeply than your knife cut me. I know you, Brutus. You really did – do – love her. You would not have wanted her to live an unhappy life. Especially one with you. Had I presented you

the choice, you would have given her up willingly. Sacrifice is in your nature. But the blow would have been close to mortal. So I chose for you. For that, I ask your forgiveness.

BRUTUS
With her, I was always the person I dreamed I'd be. My life would have been so different...

CAESAR
We don't know that. We are who we are.

BRUTUS
But not who we claim to be. Who we want to be. Poor, poor Portia. She loved me too much, that's her tragedy. I think she knew I'd lost my only...

CAESAR
We both lost her. Daughter and sister, wife and mother. She was all these, and we all lost her. Pompey, too.

BRUTUS
If she was ever ours. We had that in common. Why didn't we ever talk of it? It was a wall between us. It should have been a bridge. We, who loved her best.

CAESAR
Now she belongs to neither of us.

BRUTUS
At least you gave her happiness. I gave her nothing but sorrow.

CAESAR
Her happiness was your sole desire. Whereas I did only what I thought necessary.

**BRUTUS**
I thought motives didn't matter.

**CAESAR**
They matter to us. Can you forgive me?

**BRUTUS**
What happens if I say no?

**CAESAR**
There are no consequences. It is just a choice. The gods will not punish you. The hardest thing is to live with the choice once it's made.

**BRUTUS**
Then this once, I choose to be the man I say I am. Caesar, I forgive you. With all my heart. *(beat)* Do you--?

**BRUTUS**
Nothing to forgive, my son.

*A bugle sounds.*

**BRUTUS**
Dawn. The armies will be in place. Soon I'll be facing another Caesar. One I do not love half so well.

**CAESAR**
Love. You know, of course, why Roma's secret name goes unspoken. Because it is so powerful. Roma. Reverse the letters. A. M. O. R.

**BRUTUS**
*Amor.* Love.

**CAESAR**
When you killed me, you did it with love - for me, for Rome. So long as such love exists, so shall Roma.

*Slowly, Brutus holds out his arms.*

CAESAR
My son.

*They embrace. A series of images flash around them, of war, of loss, of BRUTUS killing himself, the ghost of Caesar watching ominously. The sounds of marching and orders, then horses, steel on steel, cannons, gunfire, aircraft strafing, and explosions. Then silence.*

ANTONY (V.O.)
This was the Noblest Roman of them all:
All the Conspirators save only he
Did that they did in envy of great Caesar.
He only, in a general honest thought
And common good to all, made one of them.
His life was gentle, and the Elements
So mix'd in him that Nature might stand up
And say to all the world 'This was a man!'

THE END

## PLAYWRIGHT'S NOTES

It's hard to think of any historical figure more redeemed with the stroke of a playwright's pen than Brutus. Before Shakespeare's play, he lived in an icy lake at the bottom of Hell. In *The Inferno*, Dante gives Lucifer three mouths, allowing the Devil to chew forever history's greatest betrayers: Judas Iscariot, Caius Cassius, and Brutus. Right through the Renaissance, Brutus was a villain, the treasonous coward who killed perhaps the greatest military and political leader the world had ever known.

Yet, in an act of brazen daring, Shakespeare turns Brutus into a hero.

We all agree that Shakespeare's play is Brutus' story. For a piece entitled THE LIFE AND DEATH OF JULIUS CAESAR, it's astonishing how little of Caesar there actually is — no Consulship, no pirate ship, no Gaul, no Civil War, no Pompey, no Cleopatra. We pick up at the end of the dictatorship, mere days before his death. Alas, Caesar was far too successful in his life to be made into a tragic hero. So Shakespeare, in his brilliance, turns 1600 years of history on its head, transforming Caesar into a half-deaf epileptic narcissist. Instead he makes his play about Brutus, the honorable man. It is incedibly subversive, a remarkable feat of daring.

If there is one glaring dramatic fault in Shakespeare's JULIUS CAESAR, it is the lack of interaction between Brutus and Caesar themselves. Shakespeare's audience was much more knowledgeable about Roman history, so he could take for granted that the nuances would be understood. Today we are not so well informed of the great and twisted personal relationship these men had. We do not know why Brutus repeatedly says he loves Caesar, nor do we see how they got to the point where murder is necessary, where Brutus believes that it indeed 'must be by his death.'

As I am always drawn to gaps in stories, this was a siren's call I could not resist.

Like everyone else, I learned about Brutus and Caesar from Shakespeare. What a reveleation it was when, on a car trip with my father, I listened to an audiobook of *The First Man In Rome* by Colleen McCullough. Her research is so thorough, her characterizations so mesmerizing, I found myself forevermore fascinated with all things Roman. If I learned about Brutus and Caesar from Shakespeare, I learned about Rome from McCullough. My take on the people, customs, and times are greatly influenced by her excellent series of books. She has been accused of admiring Caesar too much, a fault shared by the vast majority of Romans, both then and now (to say nothing of kings, tsars, princes, and emperors throughout history - and also, apparently, Alexander Hamilton).

Reading McCullough sent me off on an exploration of Plutarch, Suetonius, Livy and the rest. As I delved further and further into history, I began to resent Shakespeare for his treatment of Caesar. Like McCullough and so many others before me, I grew to admire and respect this amazing man. And I began to look at the play, not in terms of what is in it, but what is left out of it.

One set of circumstances I've consciously adopted from her books for dramatic effect. She was the first writer I know to suggest Brutus was engaged to Caesar's daughter. Caesar's affair with Brutus' mother is fact. But for me, using Julia as a stand-in for Roma herself was just too apt to ignore. And it makes a two-hour play about politics more tolerable.

    For the rest, I've tried to straddle the gap between history and Shakespeare. No, Antony never gave the famous oration. Instead he passed a pardon for Brutus and the others. But the fact remains that when the tide of public opinion turned, Antony turned with it. That he was a follower and not a leader does not affect this play. As I do far worse things to him here, I do make reference to his speech to the Plebs. It's the least I can do.

    Naturally, there is an ongoing echo of Roman times in Western culture. We've seen it time and again, and are in the midst of it now. I did not set out to write a polemic on modern politics, but in the readings and public performances, I've heard the audience laughter and understood that they were hearing strong resonances with our current times. To which I can only say, we modeled ourselves on Rome. Should be be surprised when we act out their rise and fall? Those who fail to study history are doomed to repeat it.

◆ ◊ ◆

    I owe many personal thanks:

    To Ed, Grant, Mike and the rest of the cast, for breathing such life into the roles. And to Joe and Bonnie, for welcoming us in to play on their stage.

    To Rob Kauzlaric, who after playing the role on and off for a decade with me will always be the voice of Brutus in my head.

    To my wife Jan, who let me direct CAESAR a decade ago and ever since has helped me explore both Rome and Shakespeare, in words and in person.

    Most of all, to Rick Sordelet, my partner in crime and best of friends, for wanting to take the random misfires of my brain and turn them into art. Thank you.

Ave,<br>DB

## ABOUT THE PLAYWRIGHT

David Blixt is an acclaimed author and actor living in Chicago. An Artistic Associate of the Michigan Shakespeare Festival, where he is the resident Fight Director, he is also co-founder of A Crew Of Patches Theatre Company, a Shakespearean repertory based in Chicago. He has acted and done fight work for the Goodman Theatre, Chicago Shakespeare Theatre, Steppenwolf, the Shakespeare Theatre of Washington DC, First Folio Shakespeare, and the Performance Network, among many others.

As a writer, his STAR-CROSS'D series of novels place the characters of Shakespeare's Italian plays in their historical setting, drawing in figures such as Dante, Giotto, and Petrarch to create an epic of warfare, ingrigue, and romance. In HER MAJESTY'S WILL, Shakespeare himself becomes a character as Blixt explores Shakespeare's "Lost Years," teaming the young Will with the dark and devious Kit Marlowe to hilarious effect. In the COLOSSUS series, Blixt brings first century Rome and Judea to life as he relates the fall of Jerusalem, the building of the Colosseum, and the coming of Christianity to Rome.

His first plays were original adaptations of classic tales for Ann Arbor's Junior Theatre, including Robin Hood, The Prince and the Pauper, and the Arabian Nights. After a dozen years of writing novels, the idea for EVE OF IDES brought him back to writing for theatre, hopefully for good.

## David Blixt's Novels
## From SORDELET INK

### The Star-Cross'd Series

### The Master Of Verona
### Voice Of The Falconer
### Fortune's Fool
### The Prince's Doom

### The Colossus Series

### Colossus: Stone & Steel
### Colossus: The Four Emperors

*and coming Winter 2014*

### Colossus: Wail of the Fallen
### Colossus: Triumph of the Jews

### Her Majesty's Will

Visit
WWW.DAVIDBLIXT.COM
for more information.